Building Decentralized Blockchain Applications

Learn How to Use Blockchain as the Foundation for Next-Gen Apps

Shahid Shaikh

www.bpbonline.com

FIRST EDITION 2021
Copyright © BPB Publications, India
ISBN: 978-93-89898-620

All Rights Reserved. No part of this publication may be reproduced or distributed in any form or by any means or stored in a database or retrieval system, without the prior written permission of the publisher with the exception to the program listings which may be entered, stored and executed in a computer system, but they can not be reproduced by the means of publication.

LIMITS OF LIABILITY AND DISCLAIMER OF WARRANTY
The information contained in this book is true to correct and the best of author's & publisher's knowledge. The author has made every effort to ensure the accuracy of these publications, but cannot be held responsible for any loss or damage arising from any information in this book.

All trademarks referred to in the book are acknowledged as properties of their respective owners but BPB Publications cannot guarantee the accuracy of this information.

Distributors:

BPB PUBLICATIONS
20, Ansari Road, Darya Ganj
New Delhi-110002
Ph: 23254990/23254991

DECCAN AGENCIES
4-3-329, Bank Street,
Hyderabad-500195
Ph: 24756967/24756400

MICRO MEDIA
Shop No. 5, Mahendra Chambers,
150 DN Rd. Next to Capital Cinema,
V.T. (C.S.T.) Station, MUMBAI-400 001
Ph: 22078296/22078297

BPB BOOK CENTRE
376 Old Lajpat Rai Market,
Delhi-110006
Ph: 23861747

To View Complete
BPB Publications Catalogue
Scan the QR Code:

Published by Manish Jain for BPB Publications, 20 Ansari Road, Darya Ganj, New Delhi-110002 and Printed by him at Repro India Ltd, Mumbai

www.bpbonline.com

Dedicated to

*Satoshi Nakamoto,
The Inventor of Bitcoin and Blockchain*

About the Author

Shahid Shaikh is a software architect with 6+ years of experience working with emerging technologies. He is also an author and has written three books, and he is an active open source contributor. He has expertise in Blockchain, distributed systems, and software architecture.

Apart from writing code and authoring books, he is a vintage bike enthusiast and rides his vintage Royal Enfield across various locations. He has a keen interest in carbon-free energy generation, space exploration, and electric vehicles.

About the Reviewer

Rahil is a computer engineer and is currently working as the VP of Architecture and Blockchain in one of India's leading Cryptocurrency exchanges.

He is currently helping his company implement and scale their Blockchain and Exchange technology.

Rahil completed his Bachelors in Engineering from Mumbai University in 2013 and has over 6 years of experience in working with emerging technologies, including Blockchain. He is highly passionate about Blockchain. He believes that Bitcoin and other decentralized systems are going to change the world for the better, and they are absolutely the best way forward.

Rahil is also the creator of **ciphertrick.com** and the "**The getting started programmer**" Youtube channel, where he regularly shares his knowledge with the community.

He lives with his wife and family in Mumbai. You can reach out to him on twitter; his Twitter handle is **@rahil471**.

LinkedIn Profile:

https://www.linkedin.com/in/rahil-shaikh-38675978/

Check out his latest video course on Deno:

https://www.youtube.com/playlist?list=PL5YcOcm9rSqzUThvf1oHgx2EqLqlW-0vn

Acknowledgement

There are a few people I want to thank for their continued and ongoing support while I was writing this book. First and foremost, I would like to thank my family for putting up with me while I was spending many weekends and evenings on writing—I couldn't have completed this book without their support.

I would also like to thank Rahil for providing his insight with a technical review of this book.

Finally, I would like to thank the entire BPB Publications team for giving me the opportunity to write this book.

Preface

Bitcoin, upon its inception in 2008, took the financial world by storm. It became the first alternative to the debt-based paper currency. Bitcoin is powered by the underlying technology that shocked the technology world. The core technology was named **Blockchain** - immutable proof of records linked together in a chain and distributed across every peer in the world.

This simple yet powerful concept opens a new branch in the computing world. Blockchain is being conceptualized to be used in sectors like supply chain, medical records, and land records.

I ventured into blockchain and cryptocurrency in early 2015. To learn more about it, I joined one of India's largest crypto exchanges and helped them build and scale their infrastructure. I gained treasure knowledge while working on the exchange.

One of the branches of Blockchain is the decentralized application. This is the new set of applications that offer alternatives to the traditional client/server model of web development. Using this approach, developers can build next-generation applications with the core blockchain technology.

Decentralized applications are slowly venturing into the real-world applications, and this was my motivation to author this book—to provide in-depth information and knowledge about Blockchain and decentralized application to the readers.

Chapter 1 discusses blockchain and explains the core technologies that power the blockchain. We will also learn about Bitcoin and how it works in depth.

Chapter 2 looks at the Ethereum and smart contracts in detail. The smart contract is the turing complete programming language to build the application that can be executed on the Ethereum blockchain.

Chapter 3 helps you learn about interplanetary file systems and how to use them to build decentralized applications. IPFS is the ground breaking technology to build next-generation blockchain applications.

Chapter 4 introduces the first decentralized database of this book—OrbitDB. It is a serverless peer-to-peer decentralized database software that runs on top of IPFS. OrbitDB provides easy-to-use APIs to help developers integrate and build applications.

Chapter 5 discusses the BigchainDB—a blockchain based database. BigchainDB is an asset-focused database that provides all the blockchain features, along with modern database capabilities such as indexing, querying, and processing.

Chapter 6 explores the TiesDB—a blockchain-based mutable database. TiesDB provides all the database features of a modern database.

Chapter 7 walks you through the Bluzelle—a decentralized tamper proof database with byzantine fault tolerance.

Chapter 8 reviews the Amazon Quantum ledger database—QLDB. Amazon QLDB is a cloud-based database solution that offers ledger-based record management.

Chapter 9 talks about the OpenBazaar—Decentralized Ecommerce solution. OpenBazaar is a decentralized application built for the general public to create their own Ecommerce store.

Chapter 10 introduces the DTube—a decentralized version of Youtube. We will look at how DTube works and its architecture, along with how we can use it to host and share videos.

Chapter 11 takes you through the Ocean protocol—a decentralized data exchange protocol.

Downloading the code bundle and coloured images:

Please follow the link to download the
Code Bundle and the *Coloured Images* of the book:

https://rebrand.ly/tjdk5zf

Errata

We take immense pride in our work at BPB Publications and follow best practices to ensure the accuracy of our content to provide with an indulging reading experience to our subscribers. Our readers are our mirrors, and we use their inputs to reflect and improve upon human errors if any, occurred during the publishing processes involved. To let us maintain the quality and help us reach out to any readers who might be having difficulties due to any unforeseen errors, please write to us at :

errata@bpbonline.com

Your support, suggestions and feedbacks are highly appreciated by the BPB Publications' Family.

Did you know that BPB offers eBook versions of every book published, with PDF and ePub files available? You can upgrade to the eBook version at www.bpbonline.com and as a print book customer, you are entitled to a discount on the eBook copy. Get in touch with us at :

business@bpbonline.com for more details.

At **www.bpbonline.com**, you can also read a collection of free technical articles, sign up for a range of free newsletters, and receive exclusive discounts and offers on BPB books and eBooks.

BPB is searching for authors like you

If you're interested in becoming an author for BPB, please visit **www.bpbonline.com** and apply today. We have worked with thousands of developers and tech professionals, just like you, to help them share their insight with the global tech community. You can make a general application, apply for a specific hot topic that we are recruiting an author for, or submit your own idea.

The code bundle for the book is also hosted on GitHub at **https://github.com/bpbpublications/Building-Decentralized-Blockchain-applications**. In case there's an update to the code, it will be updated on the existing GitHub repository.

We also have other code bundles from our rich catalog of books and videos available at **https://github.com/bpbpublications**. Check them out!

PIRACY

If you come across any illegal copies of our works in any form on the internet, we would be grateful if you would provide us with the location address or website name. Please contact us at:
business@bpbonline.com with a link to the material.

If you are interested in becoming an author

If there is a topic that you have expertise in, and you are interested in either writing or contributing to a book, please visit **www.bpbonline.com**.

REVIEWS

Please leave a review. Once you have read and used this book, why not leave a review on the site that you purchased it from? Potential readers can then see and use your unbiased opinion to make purchase decisions, we at BPB can understand what you think about our products, and our authors can see your feedback on their book. Thank you!

For more information about BPB, please visit **www.bpbonline.com**.

Table of Contents

1. **Introduction to Blockchain and Decentralized Network 1**
   Structure 1
   Objective 1
   Introduction to Blockchain 2
   What is Blockchain? 3
   Types of Blockchain 4
   Public Blockchain 5
   Federated (Consortium) Blockchain 5
   Private Blockchain 5
   History of Blockchain 6
   Blockchain Core Components 7
   Node 8
   Transaction 8
   Block 9
   Chain 10
   Miners 11
   Consensus 12
   Proof of Work 13
   Proof of Stake 13
   Byzantine Fault Tolerance 14
   Bitcoin 14
   How Bitcoin Works? 15
   What is a Double Spending Issue? 17
   Blocks 19
   Merkle Tree 19
   Bits 21
   Nonce 22
   Transactions 22

	TXID	23
	Transaction Data	24
	Fees	24
	Weight	25
	UTXO	25
	Blockchain and Decentralization	26
	Decentralized Application	27
	Working of Decentralized Apps or DApps	28
	DApps Protocols	29
	Networking Layer	31
	Data Definition and Naming Layer	32
	Data Layer	32
	Conclusion	33
	References	33
2.	**Ethereum, Smart Contracts, and DApps**	**35**
	Structure	35
	Objective	36
	What is Ethereum?	36
	Bitcoin and Ethereum	37
	History of Ethereum	38
	Ethereum's Components	39
	Ethereum and DApps	40
	Ethereum Clients - Becoming a 'Peer'	41
	Ethereum Networks	42
	Installing Geth	42
	Synchronizing the Testnet Blockchain	44
	Installing Ganache	45
	Infura	46
	JSON RPC API	48
	Smart Contracts and Solidity Language	50
	Solidity Data Types	51
	Contract Structure	52

- State Variables 53
- Functions 53
- Function Modifier 53
- Events 54
- Struct 54
- Enum 54
- Writing Our First Solidity Program 54
- Decentralized Apps (DApps) Using Ethereum 59
- DApps Stack 62
- Front-end 62
- Smart Contracts (Backend of the App) 62
- Storage 63
- IPFS 64
- Swarm 64
- Decentralized Message Communications Protocols 66
- Conclusion 66

3. Interplanetary File System 67
- Structure 67
- Objective 67
- Introduction to IPFS 68
- How IPFS works 68
- Content-based Addressing 69
- Direct Acyclic Graph 70
- Distributed Hash Table 70
- Installing and Configuring IPFS 71
- IPFS Command Line 75
- Configuring IPFS Node 76
- Addresses 77
- Bootstrap 77
- Hosting a Static Website in IPFS 78
- Building a Full-stack App Using IPFS in the Backend 84
- IPFS Cluster 92

Libp2p 93
Transport Layer Protocol 93
End-to-end Encryption 94
    Identity Module 94
    Routing 94
    Content Discovery 94
Messaging Module 94
Conclusion 98
References 98

Decentralized Databases 99

4. **OrbitDB - Peer to Peer Distributed Database** 101
Structure 101
Objective 101
Introduction to OrbitDB 102
Installing OrbitDB 103
OrbitDB Data Models 104
Log 104
Feed 104
Key-value 105
Docs 106
Counter 107
Building DApps using OrbitDB 107
Technologies 110
Architecture 110
Conclusion 121

5. **BigchainDB** 123
Structure 123
Objective 123
Introduction to BigchainDB 124
Decentralization 125
Immutability 125

- Owner-controlled Assets 126
- High Transaction Rate 127
- Low Latency and Fast Finality 127
- Indexing and Querying Structured Data 127
- BigchainDB Use Cases 128
- Supply Chain 128
- Intellectual Property Rights Management 129
- Identity 129
- Internet of Things 129
- Data Governance 130
- Audit Trails 130
- Running a BigchainDB Node 130
- Conclusion 132

6. TiesDB 133
- Structure 133
- Objective 133
- Introduction to TiesDB 134
- Features of TiesDB 134
- Verified Identification 135
- Special Data Organization 135
- Incentive Schemes 135
- Security 135
- TiesDB Use Cases 135
- Distributed Datastore 136
- File Sharing 136
- Mass Media 136
- Intellectual Property Rights 136
- Social Networks 137
- Big Data 137
- Running a TiesDB Node 137
- Conclusion 139

7. **Bluzelle** 141
    Structure 141
    Objective 142
    Introduction to Bluzelle 142
    Features of Bluzelle 142
    Decentralized 143
    Mutable 143
    Global Coverage 143
    Affordable 143
    Shared Revenue Model 144
    Bluzelle Technology 144
    Database Engine 144
    Consensus Engine 145
    Nodes 145
    Zone 145
    Bluzelle Tokens 145
    Client Library and Proxy 146
    Bluzelle Use Cases 146
    Prediction Markets 146
    Currency exchange markets 146
    Data Streaming Networks 146
    Setting Up a Bluzelle Node 147
    Conclusion 148

8. **Amazon QLDB** 149
    Structure 149
    Objective 149
    What is Amazon QLDB? 150
    Features of Amazon QLDB 151
    Ledger Database 151
        Immutable 151
        Cryptographically Secure 152
        SQL Compatible Query Language 152

	High Availability	152
	Enterprise-grade	152
	Amazon QLDB Use Cases	153
	Finance	153
	Manufacturing	153
	Insurance	153
	Payroll Systems	153
	Supply Chain	154
	How to Use Amazon QLDB	154
	Amazon QLDB Drivers	157
	Conclusion	158
	Decentralized Apps and Frameworks	**159**
9.	**OpenBazaar**	**161**
	Structure	161
	Objectives	161
	Introduction to OpenBazaar	162
	Features of OpenBazaar	162
	Commission-free	163
	Easy to Set Up	163
	Search	163
	Built-in Bitcoin Payment Support	163
	Conflict Resolution Using Mutually Agreed on Escrow	163
	Built-in Inventory Management	164
	Multiple Shipping Options	164
	Order Management	164
	Built-in Live Chat	164
	How to Install OpenBazaar	164
	Conclusion	166
10.	**DTube**	**167**
	Structure	167
	Objective	167

Introduction to DTube 168
Steem Blockchain 168
Features of DTube 169
DTube Architecture 169
Front-end 170
Distributed Blockchain Database 170
Media Storage 170
How DTube Works 170
Conclusion 171

11. **Ocean Protocol** 173
    Structure 173
    Objective 173
    Introduction to Ocean Protocol 174
    Use Cases of Ocean Protocol 174
    Autonomous Vehicles 174
    Medical Research 175
    Global Datastore 175
    How Does Ocean Protocol Work? 175
    Data Providers 175
    Data Marketplace 176
    Data Consumer 176
    Ocean Protocol Architecture 177
    Tier 1 177
    Tier 2 177
    Tier 3 178
    Conclusion 178

Index 179-185

CHAPTER 1
Introduction to Blockchain and Decentralized Network

Blockchain is a cryptographically secure chain of records linked together and replicated across several peers around the world. Blockchain works with various underlying technologies such as immutable Merkletree, hashing, decentralized networking, replication, and so on.

Structure

In this chapter, we will cover the following topics:
- Introduction to Blockchain
- Types of Blockchain
- History of Blockchain
- Blockchain core components
- Consensus mechanism

Objective

After reading this chapter, you should be able to:

- Understand the working of Blockchain
- Know how Blockchain works
- Know the various types of Blockchain
- Understand how consensus is reached in a decentralized network
- Understand decentralization

Let's begin.

Introduction to Blockchain

"The Times 03/Jan/2009 Chancellor on the brink of second bailout for banks."

Figure 1.1

On 3 January 2009, *Satoshi Nakamoto* mined the first-ever block of Bitcoin—a peer-to-peer decentralized cryptocurrency—and added the headline of The Times as a message in the block.

You might be wondering why this message is the first phrase of the book? This is because the message is marked in history as the day when the revolution in the century-old finance industry began.

In this chapter, we will study, in brief, the history of *Blockchain* and *Bitcoin*. We will also dive into the secret life of *Satoshi Nakamoto*, the creator of Blockchain, and distributed ledger technology and Bitcoin.

We will also learn about the different types of Blockchain and their use cases. We will look at how Bitcoin works in-depth and how this decentralized network manages the most important thing in history—money.

But first, let's understand the basics of Blockchain in brief.

What is Blockchain?

Blockchain is an immutable, peer-to-peer, distributed ledger containing the records in a format called *"blocks"* that are linked together using cryptography, and hence the name Blockchain.

Blockchain is distributed, which means each computer running the program contains a copy of the entire Blockchain. It improves the reliability of the data across the network.

Blockchain is p2p based, and there is no central server required. Anyone with a computer and internet connection can become part of the network.

The distributed ledger was built for Bitcoin to handle the money aspect of the system. Ledger is a financial recording system containing the credit and debit of the particular person or account. While banks have a central ledger, Blockchain provides distributed ledger spread across thousands of machines.

Blockchain was built by Satoshi Nakamoto—a pseudonym for the programmer who built the Bitcoin, the first cryptocurrency ever. Blockchain was built to remove the *"trust"* factor from the system and allows computers to send/receive money.

Blockchain is linked using cryptographic functions. Each block in a chain knows the address of the previous block till the **Genesis block.**

> **Tip: The genesis block is the first block that is not mined but hardcoded in the system. You can check the Genesis block code here: Genesis block code.**

Blockchain stores the blocks that consist of transactions. Once the entry is made in the Blockchain, it can't be reversed, so it is immutable. In the upcoming section, we will learn how the entry of blocks is done in the chain.

The key characteristics of Blockchain are as follows:
- Immutability
- Cryptographic
- Decentralization
- Provenance
- Anonymity
- Transparency

One of the key characteristics of the Blockchain is immutability. Once data is submitted in the chain and has been confirmed by 51% of the peers in the network, you can never alter it.

Blockchain is cryptographically secure and uses **asymmetric cryptography**, where only an intended party with the key can decrypt and see the data.

Blockchain is decentralized, which means there is no central authority controlling the network. It's controlled by the participants of the network.

Blockchain provides the record of ownership. So, it supports true provenance.

Blockchain provides true anonymity to the end user. No user information such as name, IP, and location is stored in the chain, ensuring zero chances of censorship and tracking.

Blockchain is transparent. You can view every transaction since its origin to date on your browser. Everything is available to the public with no hidden agenda!

Before we proceed further, let's look at the types of Blockchain.

Types of Blockchain

Blockchain was meant to be a public ledger. However, due to corporations not wanting to share their data with the public, some Blockchains are intended to serve such entities.

Blockchain, in a nutshell, can be divided into three groups:
- Public Blockchain
- Federated (or Consortium) Blockchain
- Private Blockchain

Let's learn about them in brief.

Public Blockchain

A public Blockchain, as the name suggests, is public; so, anyone can join the Blockchain network, read the data, and write to it.

The Bitcoin network is among the first few public Blockchains in the world. You might be wondering how it's secure if it's completely open to the public.

Well, it's a valid question.

A public Blockchain such as Bitcoin has a consensus mechanism that ensure that the network is secure and data is valid across every peer connected to the system. The second part is the encryption mechanism used by Bitcoin is asymmetric, so it needs the key of the sender and receiver both to decrypt the data, which makes it secure and fraud-proof.

The consensus mechanisms used by the public Blockchain can vary between proof of work, proof of stake algorithms. We will understand the consensus system in the next section.

Public Blockchains are slower and less efficient than private and federated ones.

Federated (Consortium) Blockchain

Federated blockchains are shared Blockchain among various federations or entities. In simple words, instead of going public, the Blockchain is only shared among a few organizations.

Every read and write operation can be done only using the permissions granted by the authorities. As it has fewer peers, a federated Blockchain is fast and efficient as compared to a public Blockchain.

A federated Blockchain does not require any consensus algorithm to handle conflict issues as all the peers in the Blockchain network are identified.

Private Blockchain

Private Blockchain, as the name suggests, is used only by the organization. It's not shared with anyone and is only used within the network. Private Blockchains do not use any consensus to solve conflict issues as it's predefined in the system. Only selected peers can insert a block in the network.

We have studied the Blockchain and its types; now, let's understand the history of Blockchain.

History of Blockchain

The core principles of Blockchain—distributed computing, cryptography, decentralization, and consensus algorithms—are not new. They have been around since the 90s and are taught in computer science classes all around the world.

So, one may ask why distributed ledgers technology and Blockchain came into existence in 2009.

Well, to find the answer to this, we must understand how our banking system works. Banks are the central authority that owns your money and keeps a record of every transaction you make.

There was a time when paper currency was printed based on the number of natural resources one country possesses, mainly gold and silver. It's unlikely that we find gold and silver mines every day, so the supply was limited, and so the value of the currency.

The paper currency you currently hold is printed based on credit without the backing of natural resources such as gold and silver. This move allows federal banks to print as much money as they want.

Remember the newspaper cut on the first page? That's the time when this economic model failed and when banks closed like small shops. That was the 2008 global recession.

So, where is the problem?

Satoshi thinks it's the central authority of the banks. Satoshi had a vision of the currency supported globally and transferred anywhere without a bank. This vision later became Bitcoin.

But, is Bitcoin the first cryptocurrency ever?

The first work on cryptocurrency can be traced back to 1991 by *Stuart Haber* and *W. Scott Stornetta*. This duo wanted to develop a **cryptographically** secured document timestamp system, where the document cannot be altered once stored in the system.

They used the Merkle-tree concept to store and track the documents in the system. The major work that leads to the development of the first Blockchain is the development of hashcash - proof of work algorithm.

Hashcash was developed to prevent spams in the computing system. Later on, *Hal Finney* developed a reusable proof of work algorithm using hashcash.

Satoshi Nakamoto, in 2008, combined Merkle Trees and reusable proof of work algorithm with building his Blockchain to support the working of a new cryptocurrency.

The first-ever **Bitcoin** transaction was sent on *12 January 2009* by *Satoshi Nakamoto*, where he sent 50 Bitcoins to *Hal Finney*.

Bitcoin transactions have since reached their high to around $20000, as you can see in this graph:

Figure 1.2

At the time of writing this book, no one knew who Satoshi was—the creator of Bitcoin and Blockchain.

Now, let's understand the components of the Blockchain system.

Blockchain Core Components

Blockchain consists of the following core components:
- **Node:** Computer within the system
- **Transaction:** Actual transaction of value, the smallest component of the Blockchain
- **Block:** It's a data structure where transactions are stored in a Merkletree format.
- **Chain:** A sequence of blocks in a specific order.

- **Miners:** Specific nodes that perform the transaction and block validation
- **Consensus:** A mechanism through which networks reach the agreement

In a nutshell, here's how a Blockchain works in six steps:

1. Node submits the transaction in the network.
2. Miners pick up the transaction and keep it in the memory pool.
3. Miners add the transaction in the block.
4. Miners submit the block and compete in the network to find the hash of the block (if consensus is based on proof of work system).
5. Once the proper hash is found, the block is submitted to the network.
6. Every other node verifies the hash, and if 51% of the nodes verify and find the hash to be correct, the network reaches consensus, and the block becomes immutable.

Let's understand each component in brief.

Node

Each participant in the network is called a node. A node is a computer running the software required to join the Blockchain network.

It does require an internet connection to join and participate in the network. It can be a simple computer laptop or a huge data center.

In a public Blockchain, anyone can become a node and join the network. The number of nodes is important to make the system more secure and hard to attack.

Transaction

The transaction is the basic building block of the Blockchain. It is generated by the node and submitted in the chain, which is later picked up by the Miner and added in the block.

The transaction consists of the following information:
- ID (hash)
- Address (hash)
- Receiver (hash)
- Amount - Amount to send in crypto
- Fees - Fees to send the transaction
- Signed hash - Hash generated by the sender

There is little more information depending on the cryptocurrency, but the above-mentioned information is mandatory.

Did you notice that there is no user information stored? This is because Blockchain promises anonymity, so no information about the sender is stored except their address, which is again a hash.

Block

Block is a data structure that stores a bunch of transactions and submits it to the Blockchain for validation. If validation is successful, the block becomes immutable.

The Miner Node generates blocks. Miner Node picks up transactions from the memory pool and generates a block. This block is also called **"Candidate block."**

Every block consists of the following:
- **Block header:** Contains version, last block, time, and target
- **Nonce:** Number to consider for hash generation
- **Transactions:** List of transactions in a Merkletree format

Block header consists of critical information such as version number, last block hash, timestamp, target number, and so on.

The block is added in the chain by hashing the block header and hoping that data is less than the target number.

The target number is decided using the difficulty number. Difficulty is a number that decides the time taken by the miner to mine the block. It Should be around ~10 minutes on the Bitcoin network.

A nonce is a number that is used by the miner to generate the hash to meet the target number. The Nonce is incremented by the miner to meet the required target value.

Once the hash is found, the block is mined and submitted to the chain. Each block is linked with the previous block, forming the chain as seen in the following image:

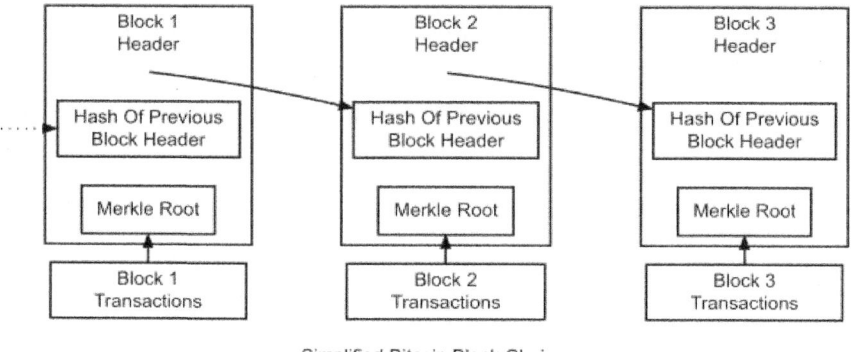

Simplified Bitcoin Block Chain

Figure 1.3

Let's proceed to the next component.

Chain

The chain is the blocks linked together using cryptography and shared across every node. Each node maintains the latest copy of the chain, forming the network of strong, reliable, and consistent nodes.

The chain consists of blocks. Blocks contain transactions, as you saw earlier. Each transaction is associated with the account, forming the ledger. Using the chain, one can determine the ledger information of the particular address and verify the transactions.

Since the chain is distributed across the network, there is no chance of fraud. If someone tries to add a false block from their machine, the network will verify and reject the block. To take over the network, one must have 51% control of the node (Hashing/Computing power of the node) in the network.

It is also called a 51% attack.

Tip: 51% attack is the distributed attack in which attackers try to control the Blockchain network by infecting and controlling hashing power of 51% of the nodes. It's nearly impossible for the network, such as Bitcoin, but it can be implemented for smaller networks.

The chain is shared across the nodes in the network in the following steps:

1. New transactions are broadcast to all nodes
2. Each node collects new transactions into a block
3. Each node works on finding a difficult proof-of-work for its block
4. When a node finds proof-of-work, it broadcasts the block to all nodes
5. Nodes accept the block only if all transactions in it are valid and not already spent
6. Nodes express their acceptance of the block by working on creating the next block in the chain, using the hash of the accepted block as the previous hash

These steps are mostly the same for the majority of the proof of the work-based system.

The chain is stored in the binary format on the nodes. Depending on the operating system and chain network, it is stored at the following location by default, and we are taking the Bitcoin chain as an example:

Linux

/home/[username]/.bitcoin/blocks/

Windows

C:\Users\[username]\AppData\Roaming\Bitcoin\

Mac

~/Library/Application Support/Bitcoin/

You can, of course, store it at different locations based on the chain configuration.

Let's proceed to one of the most important components of any chain—Miners.

Miners

Miners are the nodes that perform the process to add a new block in the chain, adding the transactions sent by the user.

Miners do this process by performing a deep level of hash calculations that takes around 10 minutes in the case of Bitcoin.

This calculation costs a lot of computing power, so it is required to pay the miners to run the operation in the surplus profit. Every time a miner performs a successful block insertion in the chain, the system rewards them with an incentive. In the case of Bitcoin, it is 12.5 Bitcoin per successful block at the time of writing this book.

So, how does mining work?

The mining process begins with building a new candidate block by picking up the transactions from the memory pool.

The candidate block contains the block header. Miners try to calculate the hash by passing the block header to the SHA256 function.

> **Tip: SHA256 is the hash function used to generate a hash based on the input.**

The hash returned should be lower than the target value defined by the system at the moment. If not, the miner increments the Nonce and calculates the hash again. This process continues until the correct hash is found. Hash is the CPU intensive process, so most miners use advanced CPUs to perform this job.

The mining process is energy dominant, so it requires lots of electricity to perform the hash calculations. Miners also collect the transaction fee provided in each transaction, plus the mining reward generated by the system.

Let's learn how consensus is being achieved in the Blockchain network.

Consensus

The consensus is the set of rules agreed by all parties of the network. There are three types of consensus algorithms used by the Blockchain networks.

- Proof of work
- Proof of stake
- Byzantine fault tolerance

Proof of work is the original consensus mechanism created by Satoshi Nakamoto for the Bitcoin cryptocurrency. Let's understand both of them in detail.

Proof of Work

Proof of work is a consensus mechanism in which one has to produce data is difficult to generate but easy to verify.

Bitcoin uses proof of work and asks miners to generate the hash, which is less than the target number. In Bitcoin, the miner has to produce a hash that starts with certain 0s. For example, if the target is 10, a miner has to produce hash starts with beginning with 0s that are less than 10.

It sounds simple, but it's extremely difficult to generate using the **SHA-256** function. Once a hash that satisfies the target is generated, all the others can verify using the target that was used to generate the hash. So, it's easy to verify but hard to generate.

Why is it so tough to generate?

To prevent spams and denial of service attacks, proof of work asks miners to invest a ton of money to build an infrastructure to perform mining, and they are rewarded by the system.

This difficulty also ensures that the false transaction does not flood the system because it will take lots of time and money to flood the system with the bad transaction; instead, one will mine and earn some good money!

Proof of Stake

Proof of work is a solid **consensus mechanism**, but it consumes a lot of computing power and energy. The energy cost to generate my blocks is so high that one can power an entire city with that energy.

Proof of work is faced with scaling issues. To solve these scaling issues, engineers across the world agreed to another form of consensus that is called **Proof of Stake (POS).**

In proof of work, when the block is about to be mined, every miner in the network tries to generate the hash to earn the reward. Ultimately, only one miner among thousands will get the hash and the reward, which, in turn, wastes the efforts of other miners.

In proof of stake, the miner/validator is chosen based on various stakes such as random, several blocks mined, and so on. So, the network chooses the miner and asks them to mine the block, giving everyone a fair chance plus saving the effort of other miners.

In proof of stake, the stake could be money, ranking, or stake itself. When a miner tries to cheat and add a bad/corrupted block in the network, the stake is slashed, or a penalty is charged against the miner.

So, how is the miner selected in proof of stake?

In general, it can be done randomly. The system picks up a random miner from the network and assigns them the block.

The network can assign a formula using which it can decide the miner when a new block is ready to mine.

Proof of stake is simple and saves lots of computational effort. Ethereum, the second most popular cryptocurrency in the world, is going to make a switch to proof of stake-based consensus from proof of work, which is their current consensus mechanism.

Let's understand another popular consensus mechanism, i.e. **Byzantine fault tolerance.**

Byzantine Fault Tolerance

Byzantine Fault Tolerance (BFT) is a consensus mechanism in a distributed system, wherein consensus is reached even if the nodes in the network fail to respond or respond with incorrect information.

BFT ensures that the system is up and running and performing its function even if the network is under attack or some technical issues occurred.

So far, we have studied the Blockchain and its components. In the next section, let's learn about cryptocurrency, which created the revolution with its technology and approach to finance.

Bitcoin

Bitcoin is the world's first peer-to-peer electronic cash system. Bitcoin offers anonymity, transparency, and no third-party dependent system to exchange value such as Money.

Satoshi Nakamoto invented Bitcoin in 2009, and it's been hailed as one of the most important inventions of the century.

Bitcoin was invented to solve trust-based dependency in the current commerce system. We as people trust banks, governments, and federal reserves to safeguard money and provide a platform for the common man to trade and exchange using the paper currency.

Due to these trust-based models, the control of the economy is in the hands of a few people, who can use it for malicious purposes. I don't want to go into detail about it because our book is not meant for bashing the banks and governments ;)

However, there was no alternative, and you had to go to the bank to handle your financial needs. Then, Bitcoin arrived as a new and better alternative.

To trade in Bitcoin, you don't need any bank or government approval. You can send money to your peers using your computer or mobile. It's as simple as that.

In this section, we will learn in-depth about how Bitcoin works, how each transaction is formed and added to the block, and how it has done more than just solving our money problems.

Note: I highly recommend our readers to print out the Bitcoin whitepaper written by Satoshi and give it a thorough read. You can download the paper from

https://bitcoin.org/bitcoin.pdf

How Bitcoin Works?

Bitcoin is a peer-to-peer electronic payment system created in 2009 by Satoshi Nakamoto. Bitcoin allows us to send money to anyone in the world, without the need for a central authority such as banks to issue accounts or process payments.

Bitcoin was created as a solution to the current financial system, where a marginal number of large corporations and banks control the financial world and the processing of transactions across the world.

It centralizes the control of finance and commerce and forces people to trust the banks to act responsibly.

And like Satoshi said in the P2P foundation.

"The central bank must be trusted not to debase the currency, but the history of fiat currencies is full of breaches of that trust."

Due to this trust issue, a major financial crisis affected the world at the end of 2007. This crisis inspired Satoshi to create Bitcoin.

Bitcoin is a computer program. You can download it precompiled, or you can download the source code from the Github and compile it yourself. Once you run the Bitcoin program on your computer, you become part of the network; you are a peer!

Once your computer becomes a part of the network, the program will connect to other computers running the same program. Once connected, computers will start sharing a file and try to sync the files with each other; this file is nothing but a Blockchain. Once your computer is up to date with the Blockchain files, you can start submitting the transaction.

Note:

It may raise a question: does everyone need to run the Bitcoin program to send/receive Bitcoin? Well, no. You can download a Bitcoin wallet and start making Bitcoin transactions. Those who wish to become a peer or miners in the network need to run the Bitcoin program:

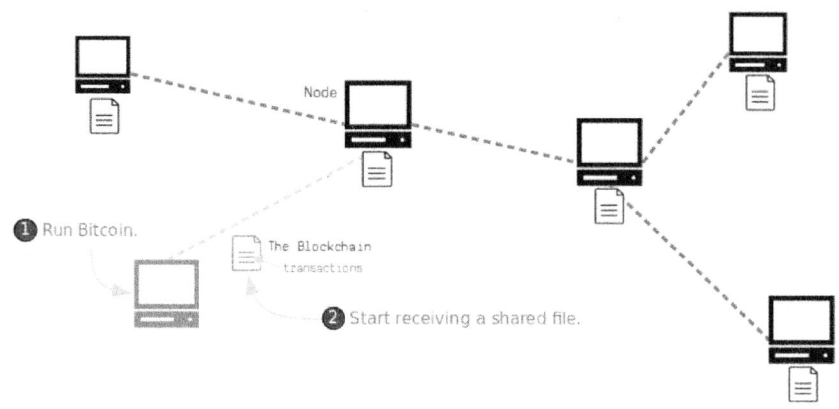

Figure 1.4

Once your computer is synced with the latest copy of the Blockchain, you are good to go. You can now submit transactions, mine the blocks, read the Blockchain, and do whatever you wish to do.

When a new transaction is submitted in the Blockchain, it is broadcast across the network. Every node then makes a copy of that transaction and adds it to their memory pool.

In the Bitcoin network, at around ~10 minutes of interval, one of the miners will mine a new block and broadcast it across the network. Every node will then update its Blockchain, and the network will be up to date:

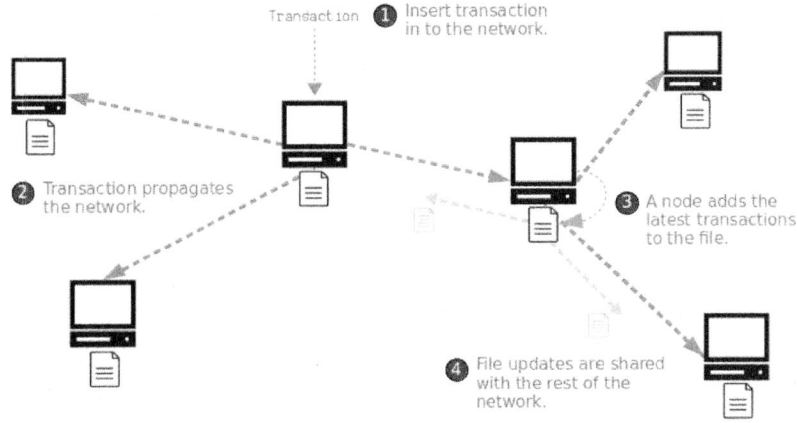

Figure 1.5

This peer-to-peer nature of the system creates a trust-free, **electronic cash system** that runs with the solid consensus mechanism.

Before we proceed ahead with the technical aspects of Bitcoin, let's understand one of the key issues that Bitcoin solved—double spending.

What is a Double Spending Issue?

Bitcoin is a peer-to-peer system, so what if two nodes submit the same transaction at the same time? How will the network with no central authority handle such a scenario? It is a serious and groundbreaking issue; let's learn how Bitcoin solved it.

Bitcoin solved this problem by introducing a memory pool. The memory pool is a buffer that every node has to maintain. Memory pool contains the transactions that are later written to the Blockchain.

When a node submits a new block, it is broadcast throughout the network:

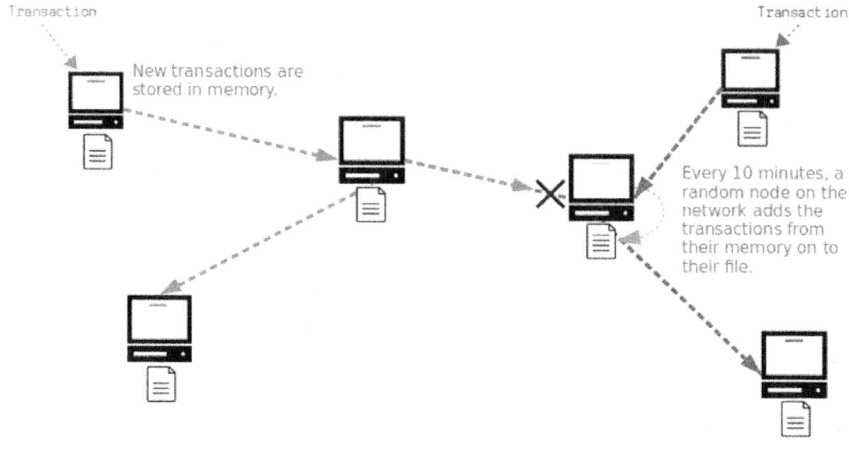

Figure 1.6

When a new block is submitted to the network, every node has to accept that as a *"correct"* transaction and remove any conflicting transaction from their memory pool.

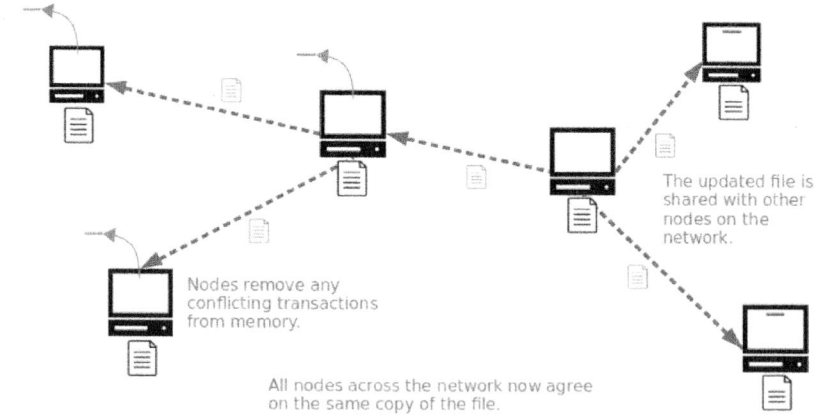

Figure 1.7

As a result, no chance of double spending can occur because it won't persist in the network if it's already been added in the block.

This double spending issue is groundbreaking and opens the way for many other projects such as Ripple cryptocurrency, which works with the current finance system but offers a solution to the double-spending.

Now, let's look over the technical aspects of Bitcoin.

Blocks

Block is the data structure that holds transactions in an immutable form. Bitcoin stores users' transactions in the blocks, and later they form a chain to build a Blockchain network.

As we discussed in the previous sections, the block is generated by the miner by the process of mining. The mining process requires a consensus algorithm to reach the agreement in the network.

Block consists of the block header, which is used by the miner to generate the hash. Block header consists of the following:

- **Version:** The version of the block
- **Previous block hash:** Hash of the last identified block, thus forming a chain
- **Merkle root:** Hash of all of the transactions in the block
- **Time:** Timestamp
- **Bits:** Hexadecimal version of the target value
- **Nonce:** Is a 32-bit random whole number that is adjusted by the miners, so that it becomes a valid number to be used to provide the hash of the block that should be less than the target hash.

The first two fields are self-explanatory, and we have already discussed them in the previous sections. Let's learn about the Merkle tree.

Merkle Tree

Merkle tree is the data structure in which every leaf node is labeled with the cryptographic hash of the data, and every non-leaf node is labeled with the hash of its child nodes, forming a tree to the root with one hash value.

As you can see in the following image, **hash 0-0** and **hash 0-1** is the hash value of data block **L1** and **L2**. Later, **Hash 0-0** and **0-1** will be hashed together to form **Hash 0** and so on until we reach a root hash:

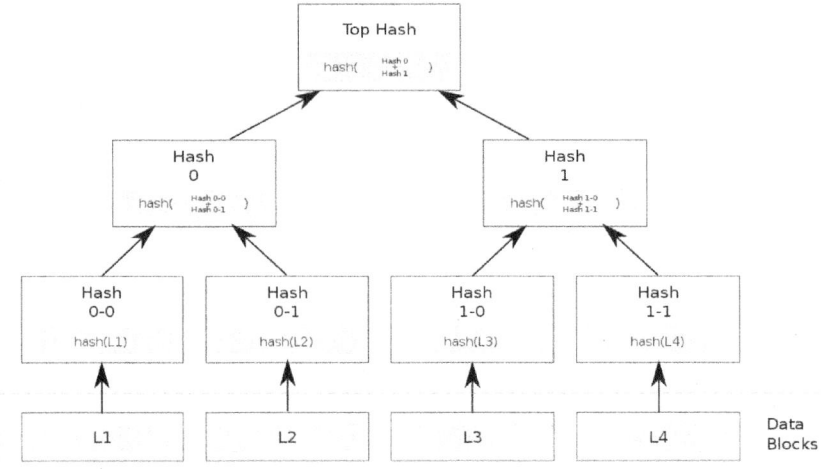

Figure 1.8

Using a Merkletree, we can generate a hash of a long series of data in a compact and secure format.

Bitcoin uses the Merkle tree to store transactions in a hashed format:

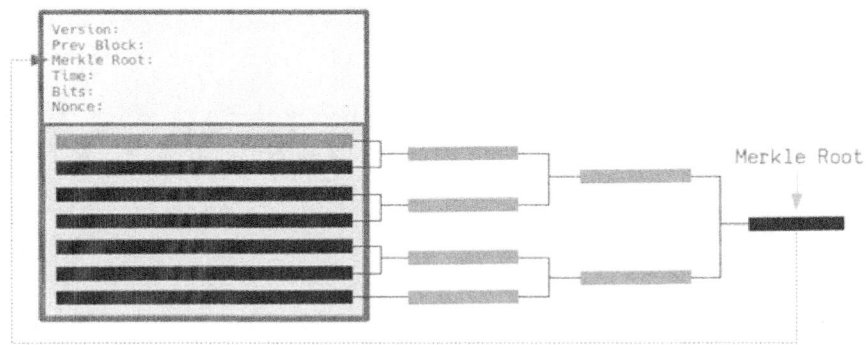

Figure 1.9

As shown in the preceding screenshot, Merkle root contains transactions that are hashed together in a way the binary tree is formed.

Merkle tree is formed by hashing the transaction IDs in a pair. Transaction IDs are used if needed, and we can perform a recheck using the transaction ID in a tree.

To generate a Merkletree, we take a pair of **transaction ID (TXID)** and hash them twice using the **SHA256** algorithm. The resulting hash is then hashed with another hashed pair twice to generate a single hash. This goes on till we generate a root hash.

Merkle trees are best suited for applications such as Bitcoin, where the size of the data matters. Due to the use of the Merkle tree, the block size is retained to 1Mb max in Bitcoin.

> **Tip:**
> **Learn in-depth about the Merkle trees; it's one of the most frequently asked questions on Facebook, Amazon, Apple, Netflix, Google (FAANG) companies. Start from here.**

http://www.mit.edu/~rio/merkle.pdf

Let's learn about the next field in the block header—Bits.

Bits

Bits is the field in the block header that stores the target value in the compact. Target is the value that is required for the miner to generate the block hash that is less than the target. We studied it in the Blockchain core concepts section.

Let's look at an example.

Here's what a target value looks like:

0x0000000000000000696f400000000000000000000000000000000000000

Storing such long values will require size, and mind you, the target will keep changing in the future.

To solve this, the target is compacted, and it looks like this in the block header field:

0x180696f4

It's easy to store and takes less size.

Here's how to decode a bit. It's divided into two parts. The first two bits after 0x represent the number of 0s in the target value, and the remaining values are appended after 0. The rest of the field is then filled with 0s till it reaches 48 bit.

So, *0x180696f4* value can be written as:

0x----18 times zero---0696f4---rest zeros----

This way, we can decode the bits in the actual target value.

In the next section, we'll look at the field, the miner used to generate the hash of the block that is lower than the target value.

Nonce

The Nonce is the field in the block header that is used by the miner to generate a hash. Bitcoin uses proof of work consensus algorithms. In proof of work, Miner has to generate a hash that is lower than the target value decided by the network.

Target value starts with several 0s, and it's really difficult to get such a hash using the **SHA256** algorithm on a random basis. So, Nonce comes into the picture, Miner uses the Nonce field to generate a hash, and if it is not lower than the target value, Miner increments the Nonce and tries again.

When the lucky number or Nonce is found, a hash is generated. Miner announces the block in the network, and every other node verifies and makes a copy of it in their Blockchain.

So, Nonce plays a crucial role in Bitcoin mining.

We have studied about the block and important block header fields, so let's move ahead and learn about Bitcoin transactions.

Transactions

When someone tries to transfer Bitcoin from one account to another, a new transaction is formed and added to the block by the miner.

The transaction contains data that is required for proper Bitcoin transfer. Transaction data consists of the amount that the user wants to send, account information such as from and to addresses, transaction information required for the network such as transaction Ids, and so on.

Transaction in Bitcoin contains the following information:
- The transaction ID is also referred widely as TXID
- Transaction data such as INPUT, OUTPUT, and so on

- Fees
- Weight
- UTXO

Let's learn about each one of them in brief.

TXID

TXID is a 32 bytes **hexadecimal number** that is referred to as transaction ID and used to identify the transaction in Bitcoin.

TXID is generated by hashing the transaction data twice using the SHA256 hashing algorithm.

Satoshi Nakamoto sent the first-ever Bitcoin transaction to Hal Finney, and the ID of the transaction is this:

f4184fc596403b9d638783cf57adfe4c75c605f6356fbc91338530e9831e9e16

You can still view this transaction in the Blockchain explorer:

https://www.blockchain.com/btc/tx/f4184fc596403b9d638783cf57adfe4c75c605f6356fbc91338530e9831e9e16:

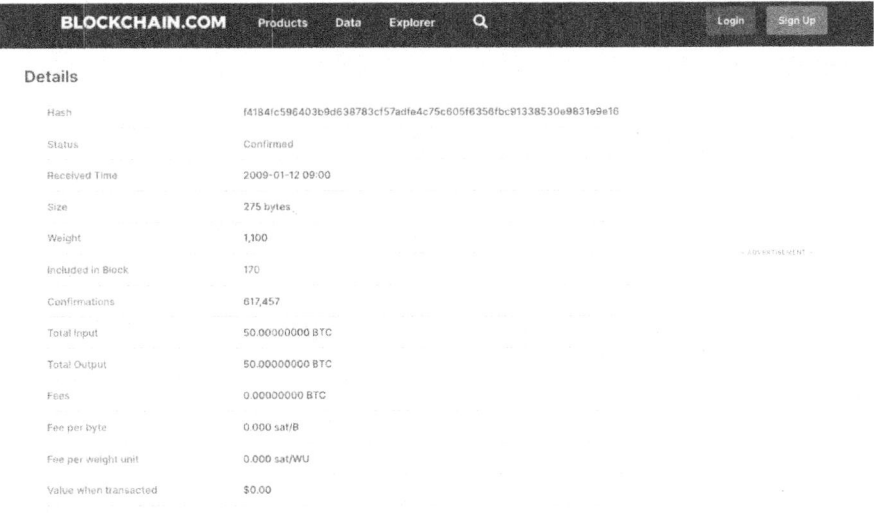

Figure 1.10

Let's look over the transaction data required to form transaction payload.

Transaction Data

Transaction data contains the information required to form INPUT and OUTPUT. Now, what are they? Well, in Bitcoin, when you send someone a few coins, you unlock a few outputs that are required and lock them again with the keys of the receiver so that only they can lock it.

Sounds confusing? Stay with me.

Let's take an example:

Imagine you have 5 Bitcoins, and you want to send 3 bitcoins to your friend. Here, 5 Bitcoins you hold is your OUTPUT, and it is split into two OUTPUT. One worth 3 Bitcoins and another worth 2 Bitcoins. The first OUTPUT will then be locked with the receiver keys so that they can unlock it. The second OUTPUT is your money, so it is again locked with your credentials for future uses.

In a nutshell, when a new transaction is formed, the whole amount is included in the **transaction payload**. It's just whatever is left is being sent back to you as an OUTPUT.

So, this approach of graph-based INPUT and OUTPUT structure provides a history of ownership of Bitcoin.

Fees

Every transaction in the Bitcoin pays some amount of money in the form of Bitcoin to the Miner. The remainder of the transaction output is also associated with the fees and paid to the miner for the work they do.

Generally, by adding lucrative fees, there is a high chance that a miner will pick your transaction from the memory pool to add into the next block. However, this is completely optional. If you don't pay the fee at the moment, it may take some time, but your transaction will be mined by some miners scattered across the world.

Here is the fee associated with the transaction. You can also check the miner award, which is 12.5 Bitcoins at the time of writing this book:

Hash	0000000000000000003ad19cc282990d349153c6f1fba702bdb6dc51eaf5dcb
Confirmations	2
Timestamp	2020-02-16 22:33
Height	617656
Miner	BTC.com
Number of Transactions	2,654
Difficulty	15,546,745,765,529.37
Merkle root	e8021d27b3bb43084de385794284794122f098afab8e872adaaccfee099f7ffd
Version	0x20400000
Bits	387,062,484
Weight	3,993,549 WU
Size	1,421,802 bytes
Nonce	1,156,369,113
Transaction Volume	7898.56822147 BTC
Block Reward	12.50000000 BTC
Fee Reward	0.26228069 BTC

Figure 1.11

Note: The remainder of the transaction is also paid to the Miner as a fee. Suppose you want to pay someone 5 Bitcoin, and you have around 10 Bitcoin in your wallet, if you don't claim the remaining 5 Bitcoin in OUTPUT section of transaction, it will be paid to the miner. It's not refundable because, well, Blockchain is immutable! So, double-check before forming a transaction payload programmatically.

Weight

As the name suggests, it refers to the size of the transaction, that is, its weight. After the introduction of weight, the transaction payload is formed by putting the validation part at the end of the payload rather than with each INPUT, as we did earlier.

UTXO

It's a short version of Unspent Transaction Output. When a new transaction is formed and new OUTPUT is generated, the one which is spent or sent to other users cannot be spent again. However, the OUTPUTs left or not spent can be used in future transactions.

These unspent outputs are called UTXOs.

UTXO is used to calculate the balance of a particular user and verify whether they have the amount to spend. UTXOs are a key part of forming new transactions and preventing double-spending.

These are the key factors that are involved in the Bitcoin transaction.

I hope you understood the concepts and the reasoning behind the technical changes done to make Bitcoin and Blockchain what they are now. In the next section, we will address one of the unique approaches to build applications that are forked from the Blockchain technology—**Decentralized Applications**.

Blockchain and Decentralization

"Cryptocurrency is a small subset of the Blockchain, like the Email of the internet."

As we studied in the previous sections, Blockchain is a peer-to-peer consensus-based network of computers. Each computer communicates with each other and exchanges data.

As there is no central authority involved in the working of Blockchain, this approach is called the *"Decentralized"* approach.

After the huge success of Blockchain technology to support the most crucial and important factor of human beings—money — engineers and technology gurus started wondering about the usage of Blockchain in other aspects of computing, such as E-commerce, hospitals, property holding, and others.

The Blockchain that is built to support Bitcoin cannot support such a wide range of data due to various reasons. Hence, it is best to build a new Blockchain-based system using the core technology behind the Blockchain built by Satoshi: decentralization, peer to peer, consensus, anonymous.

And this movement is also referred to as decentralized Web or Web 3.0, as most of these technologies will first be implemented on the Internet.

In this section, we will learn about the following:

- Decentralized application
- How does it work

- DApps technologies

Let's jump right in.

Decentralized Application

Generally, applications work on client and server models, so there is a central authority that serves those clients. As opposed to that, decentralized applications run on a peer-to-peer-based network.

Decentralized applications are already present in the market, such as **Torrent** and **Tor network**. The key change here is the data storage on the Blockchain network, which, in turn, makes it immutable, fraud-proof, and anonymous.

The decentralized application makes communication with the Blockchain deal with data. Rest everything should be the same, such as the user interface, development approach, and so on.

The front end of the decentralized application should look and work like a traditional application. The business logic, however, involves cryptography and Blockchain to deal with data generated by the application.

This is how a traditional application stack looks:

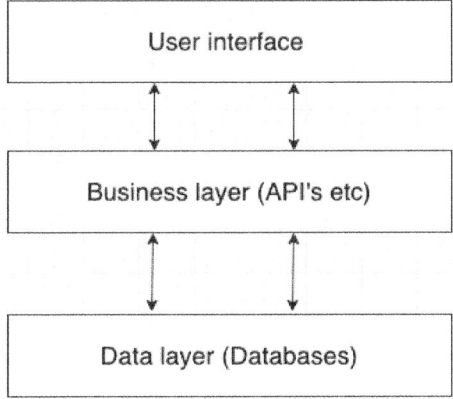

Figure 1.12

And here's how a decentralized application stack looks like:

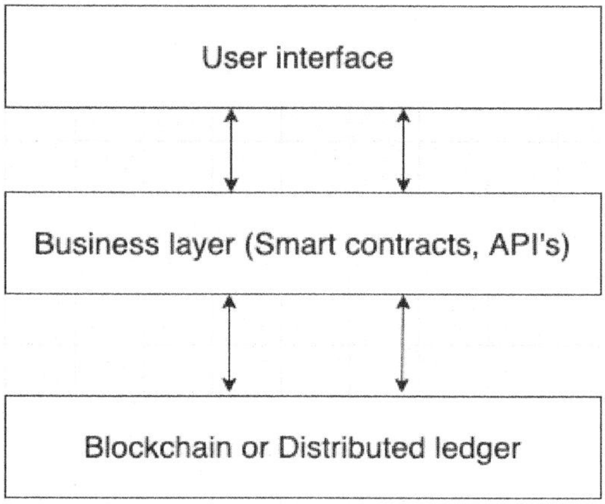

```
┌─────────────────────────────────────┐
│           User interface            │
└─────────────────────────────────────┘
                  ↕
┌─────────────────────────────────────┐
│  Business layer (Smart contracts, API's)  │
└─────────────────────────────────────┘
                  ↕
┌─────────────────────────────────────┐
│   Blockchain or Distributed ledger  │
└─────────────────────────────────────┘
```

Figure 1.13

The change is in the business layer and data layer, and we will understand the technologies being developed and used to build the business and data layer for the decentralized applications in the next section.

Working of Decentralized Apps or DApps

So, how do DApps work? There is no simple answer to this, but I will try my best to simplify it as much as possible.

So, let's learn by example.

Imagine you have an application installed on your phone, and it works like Instagram, where you can share your photos with the world.

In general, when you upload a new photo in the app, it uploads your image in some storage, makes an entry in the database, and updates the newsfeed so that everyone who follows you can see the post.

Simple, right?

Let's do the same with the help of the Blockchain.

So here, you will upload the image in the app, and it will be stored in decentralized storage such as the **Interplanetary File System (IPFS).** Storage will provide you with a hash, which is the identifier for the object.

Now, the hash would be added in the Blockchain to make a permanent entry of the photo, and then the newsfeed would be updated so that the people who follow you can see the content.

But what if you want to delete the photo? Blockchain is immutable, right? True.

In decentralized applications, every action is recorded in the chain, and even the delete action would be recorded in the chain. As mentioned earlier, you won't store actual photos in the Blockchain; instead, you will store the action, and action is immutable.

Is it simple, right?

Alright, now that you have studied what the decentralized application is and how it works, let's understand the technologies and protocols to build the decentralized application.

DApps Protocols

Bitcoin uses the Blockchain to store the actual coins, and that's pretty much it. The next big thing after Bitcoin is Ethereum, which introduced something called "smart contracts."

Smart contracts are the programs that are executed on the Ethereum Blockchain. This invention opened the path for the next-generation decentralized applications.

Ethereum saw this opportunity, and they developed a complete set of tools and protocols required to build decentralized apps on the Ethereum ecosystem.

As you can see in the following screenshot, Ethereum suits consist of Swarm, which acts as storage for the Ethereum apps, and Whisper to perform communications between the applications:

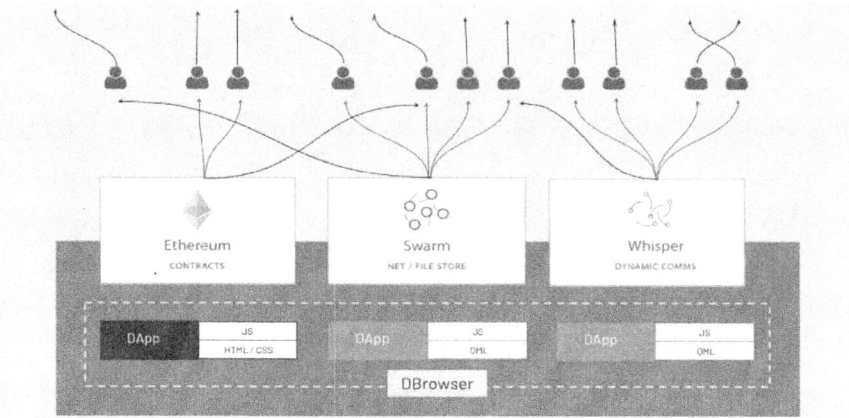

Figure 1.14

You can develop Ethereum applications using the web3.js framework. This complete ecosystem is supported by the Ethereum foundation.

The only drawback is the ecosystem itself, and you are restricted from developing and running it in the Ethereum ecosystem.

The next protocol that we will learn is completely open-source and can be used to develop decentralized applications using a mix of the technology stack.

The next protocol is a project by the *protocol.ai* team, which is called the IPFS stack. First, let's take a look at the stack:

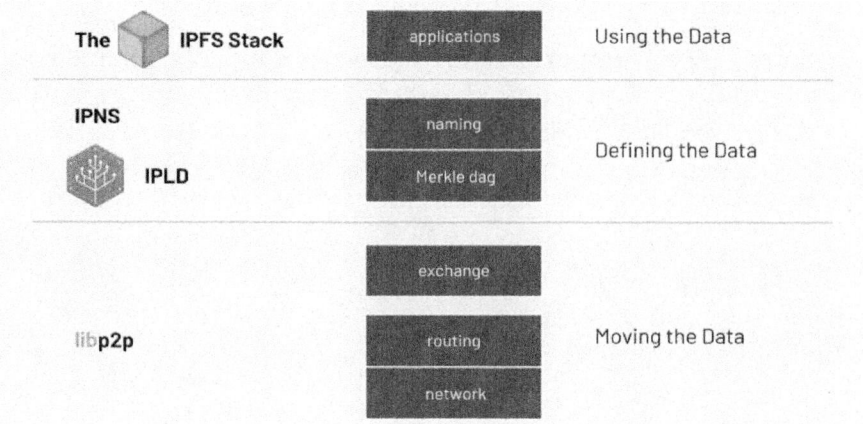

Figure 1.15

As in the preceding screenshot, the IPFS stack is divided into three subset layers:

- Networking layer
- Data definition and naming layer
- Data layer

Let's look at each substack in brief.

Networking Layer

One of the core challenges in the decentralized web is the peer-to-peer network and designing the protocols that work in a peer-to-peer network in parallel to the centralized system.

The **Libp2p** project addresses this challenge with protocols labs. Libp2p provides the modular stack that one can use to build a peer-to-peer network in conjunction with existing protocols such as **WebRTC** or any new transport layer protocols.

So, Libp2p is transported agnostics.

Features of libp2p:

- Libp2p is a modular networking stack. You can use all of it or use part of the stack to build your application.
- Libp2p provides transport and peer-to-peer protocols to build large, robust, and scalable network applications.
- Libp2p is transport protocol agnostics. It can work with TCP, UDP, WebRTC, WebSockets, and UDP.
- Libp2p offers several modules such as transport interface, discovery, distributed hash lookup, peer discovery, and routing.
- Libp2p offers built-in encryption to prevent eavesdropping.
- Libp2p offers built-in roaming features so that your service can switch networks without any intervention and loss of packets.

Libp2p is the solution upon which the networking layer of peer-to-peer can be built.

Data Definition and Naming Layer

Content addressing through hashes is widely used in a distributed system. We use hash-based content addressing in Git, cryptocurrencies, and so on. The same is also used in peer–to-peer networking.

IPLD provides a unified namespace for all hash-based protocols. Using IPLD, data can be traversed across various protocols to explore and view the data spread across a peer-to-peer network.

IPNS is a system to create a mutable address to the contents stored on IPFS. The reason why they are mutable is that the addresses of the content change every time the content changes.

Data Layer

The topmost layer in this stack is the data layer. The **IPFS** is the **peer-to-peer hypermedia protocol**. IPFS provides a way to store and retrieve data across a peer-to-peer network.

It uses IPNS and Libp2p to create, name, and distribute content across a peer-to-peer network.

Anyone can become an IPFS peer and start looking for the content using hashes. An IPFS peer does not need to store all data; they only need to store the data created by them or the data they have searched in the past.

Features of IPFS:
- IPFS provides peer-to-peer hypermedia protocols for web 3.0.
- IPFS can work with existing protocols and browsers. It gives a smooth transition from centralized web to web 3.0.
- IPFS uses Libp2p to support peer-to-peer networking.
- IPFS data is cryptographically secure.
- IPFS can save tons of bandwidth in streaming services.

IPFS is under development, and there are some great applications built by developers that are running on top of the IPFS. One of the applications of my choice is *d.tube*.

It is a decentralized version of YouTube with a built-in incentive and reward feature provided by *Steem* Blockchain.

IPFS is also trying to solve the incentive issue. We can't expect every person connected to the Internet to act as a peer. To provide an incentive to those who participate and contribute value to the network, IPFS has created a coin called Filecoin, which can be paid to peers in the network by the user.

Other projects that we will learn about in the upcoming chapters are as follows:

- **OrbitDB:** Peer-to-peer database
- **Amazon QLDB:** Distributed immutable database
- **Ocean protocol:** Data exchange protocol

These protocols provide the capability a developer needs to build a next-generation decentralized application. We will learn about these protocols in detail in the upcoming chapters.

Conclusion

We explored the Blockchain and its basic components in this chapter. We also studied Bitcoin and its working in detail, along with the way it handles double-spending issues and so on. We then moved to decentralized apps worlds and understood the protocols and frameworks required to build decentralized apps in brief.

In the next chapter, we will learn about Ethereum and its working in detail. We will also learn about the Ethereum protocols for decentralized apps.

References

- **Bitcoin official whitepaper -** https://www.bitcoin.com/bitcoin.pdf
- **P2P foundation -** https://p2pfoundation.net/
- **Satoshi Nakamoto's emails -** https://satoshi.nakamotoinstitute.org/emails/
- **Learnmeabitcoin -** http://learnmeabitcoin.com/

CHAPTER 2
Ethereum, Smart Contracts, and DApps

Ethereum is a **revolution** in the crypto world. There is no denying that. With the introduction of **smart contracts** programming language and allowing developers to build their own cryptocurrency/apps and host it on **Blockchain** were a great move and a major success.

Structure

In this chapter, we will learn about Ethereum in-depth and also cover the following topics:
- What is Ethereum?
- Bitcoin and Ethereum
- History of Ethereum
- Ethereum's components
- Ethereum and DApps
- Smart contracts and solidity language
- Decentralized Apps (DApps) using Ethereum
- DApps Stack

Objective

We will dive in-depth on each topic and cover all the details required to program the smart contract and build applications that are running on the Ethereum blockchain.

Let's learn about Ethereum!

What is Ethereum?

"Ethereum is an open-source, peer to peer, globally distributed public computing infrastructure that runs programs called smart contracts and maintains the system's state changes using the blockchain and cryptocurrency called ether."

That's a lot to take in one statement. Let's break it down, shall we?

- **Open source:** Ethereum is an open-source project. Anyone can participate and contribute to the codebase of Ethereum. Here is the codebase repository - **https://github.com/ethereum**

- **Peer to peer:** Ethereum runs on a decentralized peer-to-peer network like Bitcoin. There is no central authority to manage the conflict. Conflict is managed using consensus; we will learn about the consensus of Ethereum in the upcoming sections.

- **Globally distributed infrastructure:** Ethereum executes smart contracts on a public computing infrastructure formed using the peer-to-peer network. Think of it like a supercomputer but not in one place!

- **Smart contracts:** Smart contracts are programs that are executed on the Ethereum public distributed infrastructure. We will learn and code smart contracts in the upcoming sections.

- **Blockchain:** Ethereum uses Blockchain to store the system's state and changes to maintain a conflict-free, transparent, and decentralized system.

- **Ether:** Ether is a native coin used to charge the incentive for executing the programs on the network. It is also used to reward miners for helping mine the blocks in the network.

Ethereum is amazing. After the introduction of Bitcoin, Ethereum was the way to go when the world realized the power of Blockchain beyond finance, and it serves well. So how are Ethereum and Bitcoin different? Let's learn about it briefly.

Bitcoin and Ethereum

Ethereum shares many common elements with Bitcoin such as a peer-to-peer network, proof of work consensus algorithm to maintain conflict-free state, cryptocurrencies such as Ether to support incentive and utility payment in the network, wallets, and digital signature.

However, Ethereum differs from Bitcoin in design and purpose. While Bitcoin is designed to support the global cryptocurrency system, Ethereum is designed as a programmable virtual machine capable of executing programs on the Blockchain.

Bitcoin supports simple code execution in the form of scripts that support normal if/else statements, and Ethereum supports Turing complete programming language.

In short,

"Bitcoin is limited to cryptocurrency, Ethereum is open and general-purpose Turing complete virtual machine."

Ethereum, with its general-purpose programming language and wide range of software development kit, allows developers across the globe to build their applications. One of the famous applications is *CryptoKittie*.

CryptoKittie is a game that runs on Ethereum blockchain that allows players to buy, breed, and sell virtual cats on the Blockchain. It's extremely popular and gave the world a bird-eye view of the capability of the Blockchain.

Ethereum's scope is wide and allows developers to write their applications without the need for creating a blockchain and network by themselves. Developers can focus on building applications, while network infrastructure, state management, code execution is handled by the Ethereum network.

Let's learn a little about the history of Ethereum to understand the reason behind the invention of this amazing project.

History of Ethereum

All great innovations solve big problems, and Ethereum is no exception. Ethereum was invented at a time when people recognized the widespread application of the Bitcoin model, and we're trying to move beyond cryptocurrency.

Though it wasn't easy, developers faced a problem that required a new set of protocols and tools. They had to either build a new application on top of Bitcoin or start a new blockchain (it is a hard thing to do for every single app).

If developers choose to build on top of the Bitcoin model, they face issues, mainly technical, because Bitcoin is developed to support cryptocurrency and to move beyond it requires an immense amount of effort and probably a fork in the chain.

For projects that needed more freedom and flexibility while using Blockchain, a new blockchain was the only option. But that meant a lot of work: bootstrapping all the infrastructure elements, development, team building, testing, and so on.

In December 2013, *Vitalik Buterin*, a Russian-Canadian programmer and Bitcoin enthusiast, published a paper that coined the idea of Turing complete general-purpose Blockchain:

Figure 2.1: *Vitalik Buterin speaking at Forbes*

Here's the link to the Ethereum white paper (I recommend all of you to read it once): **https://ethereum.github.io/yellowpaper/paper.pdf**.

The idea behind Ethereum was to design a general-purpose blockchain that is programmable so that anyone around the world can program the applications and run it on the Blockchain without developing the underlying mechanisms of peer-to-peer networks, blockchains, consensus algorithms, and so on.

In July 2015, the first Ethereum block was mined. It marks the date for the general-purpose world computer to begin its work:

Figure 2.2: First Ethereum block mined (Link: **https://etherscan.io/block/0**)

Ethereum has grown to become the largest blockchain network in the world and has opened the ways for the new set of applications - decentralized apps.

In the next section, let's learn about the components of Ethereum blockchain.

Ethereum's Components

In Ethereum, following components play important roles:

- **Peer-to-peer network:** Ethereum like Bitcoin runs on themainnet network that is accessible by default at port 30303 on your computer. Ethereum Peer-to-Peer or P2P network communicates with each using a protocol called ÐΞVp2p Wire Protocol.

- **Consensus mechanism:** Ethereum uses a proof of work consensus algorithm called *Ethash POW* algorithm like Bitcoin, and they are planning to move towards proof of stake consensus mechanism shortly.
- **Transactions:** Ethereum transactions include information about the network, along with the sender, recipient, value, and payload.
- **State machine:** This is a unique and important component of the Ethereum. Ethereum state transitions are managed by Ethereum virtual machine, a virtual machine that executes bytecode generated by programs called *"smart contracts"*.
- **Data structure:** Ethereum state is also locally stored in each node. Ethereum uses the database (also called *LevelDB*), which contains the transactions and system state in a Merkle tree format.
- **Clients:** Ethereum provides several client software, such as *Go-Ethereum* also called *Geth* and *Parity*.

In the next section, we'll look at the transition of Ethereum from a general-purpose Blockchain to decentralized applications.

Ethereum and DApps

Project Ethereum started as a way to build a general-purpose blockchain that could be programmed for a variety of uses. Ethereum's vision swiftly expanded to become a platform for programming and hosting decentralized applications or DApps.

DApps portray a wider perspective than smart contracts. A DApp is, at the minimum, a smart contract and a web user interface. More broadly, a DApp is a web application that is developed on top of open, decentralized, peer-to-peer network and infrastructure.

A DApp is composed of at least:
- Smart contracts on a blockchain
- A web front-end user interface

Also, many DApps include other decentralized components, such as:
- A decentralized (P2P) storage protocol and platform such as IPFS and Swarm

- A decentralized (P2P) messaging protocol and platform such as *Libp2p* and *Whisper*

The idea and origin of DApps are aimed to take the World Wide Web to its next natural evolutionary stage, introducing decentralization with peer-to-peer protocols into every aspect of a web application. The term used to describe this evolution is web3.0, meaning the third *"version"* of the web. The world wide web controlled by no central authority.

In the next section, we will explore the capability of EthereumDApps in detail.

Let's start with the development of smart contracts before writing the smart contracts; we must learn about Ethereum clients, that is, running Blockchain in your system or using free third-party services.

Ethereum Clients - Becoming a 'Peer'

Ethereum provides client software to become a peer in the network. You can download and install these clients to become a peer and perform operations such as querying the Blockchain, performing transactions, executing smart contracts, and so on.

There are different open-source versions of Ethereum client, and they interoperate if they comply with Ethereum reference specifications and standard communication protocols. While different teams and people develop these clients, they all communicate through the standard communication protocol.

Ethereum is an open-source and community-driven project licensed under LGPL v3.0. It's free to download and can be used for any purpose. Due to these clear specifications and licensing, different projects are independently developed by the people and companies around the world.

At the time of writing this book, there are six main implementations of the Ethereum protocol written in six different programming languages:

- **Parity:** Written in Rust programming language
- **Geth:** Written in Go programming language
- **Cpp-ethereum:** Written in C++ programming language

- **Pyethereum:** Written in Python programming language
- **Mantis:** Written in Scala programming language
- **Harmony:** Written in Java programming language

We will learn about one of the most used clients—Geth—which is also a sort of official Ethereum client as the Ethereum foundation manages it.

Before running these clients in our machine, let's understand the types of Ethereum network and which one we should use.

Ethereum Networks

Ethereum networks are classified into two types:
- **Mainnet** (also known as Full node) - Live network handling real ethers, that is, money.
- **Testnet** - Test network designed for research and development.

As shown earlier, testnet is best suited for development purposes, while mainnet is the actual peer-to-peer network.

Running a **mainnet** in your machine incurs hardware resources' cost and bandwidth. I don't recommend you to run one in your local machine. You can do almost everything you need to do with the **testnet** node.

We can also use a private Blockchain like Ganache or a cloud-based client-provider such as Infura. We will learn about them also in this chapter.

So, let's install and run Geth in our machine.

Installing Geth

Geth is the Ethereum client developed in Go language that is actively developed by the Ethereum Foundation, so it is considered the "official" implementation of the Ethereum client. Generally, every Ethereum-based Blockchain will have its Geth instance running.

I am currently running Ubuntu in my machine and will install Geth in this system. If you are using Windows or macOS, you can use the following links for installation:

- Installation instruction for Windows: https://geth.ethereum.org/downloads/
- Installation instruction For Mac: https://geth.ethereum.org/docs/install-and-build/installing-geth#install-on-macos-via-homebrew

Let's install, open up a terminal, and clone the repository in your local system.

Here's the command:

`git clone` **https://github.com/ethereum/go-ethereum.git**

It may take some time to download and install Geth in your system:

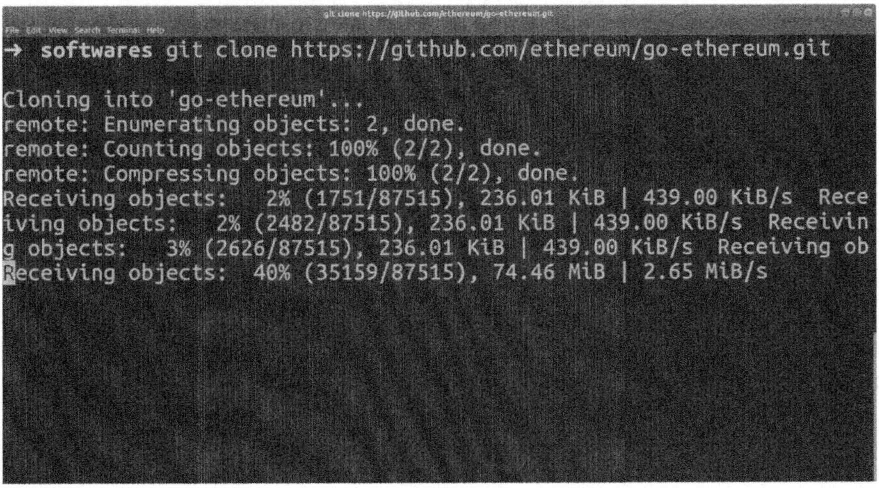

Figure 2.3

Once it is downloaded, you need to switch to the directory and run these commands:

`make geth`

It will take some time to build Geth from the source. Once installed, the executable files will be placed in the `/build/bin` folder inside the `go-ethereum` folder.

We can also directly download the build package from the website and run it on our computer. To download the build files, visit the EthereumGeth downloads page at **https://geth.ethereum.org/downloads/** and download the version suitable for your operating system. If you are a geek, build it from source, it's so satisfying :)

Once you're done building it from source or downloading and unzipping it, go to the folder and run this command to check the Geth version:

`./geth version`

It should print the Geth version details like this:

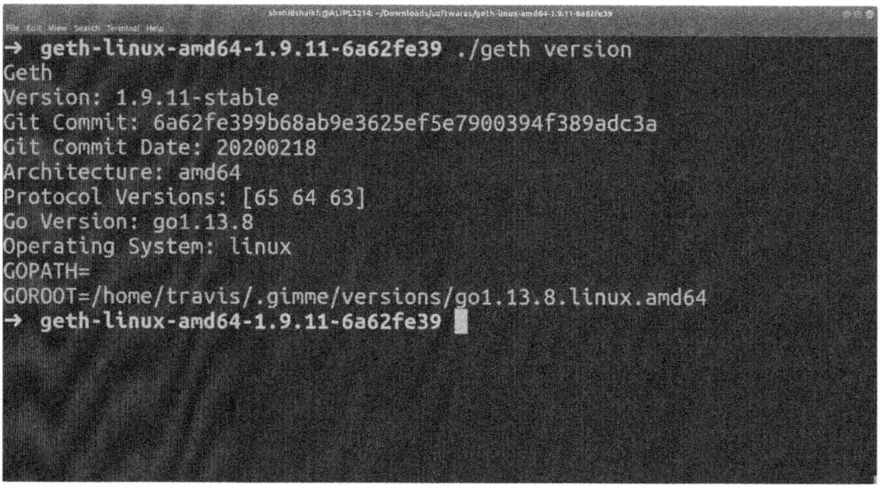

```
→ geth-linux-amd64-1.9.11-6a62fe39 ./geth version
Geth
Version: 1.9.11-stable
Git Commit: 6a62fe399b68ab9e3625ef5e7900394f389adc3a
Git Commit Date: 20200218
Architecture: amd64
Protocol Versions: [65 64 63]
Go Version: go1.13.8
Operating System: linux
GOPATH=
GOROOT=/home/travis/.gimme/versions/go1.13.8.linux.amd64
→ geth-linux-amd64-1.9.11-6a62fe39
```

Figure 2.4

You may see slightly different information than shown in the preceding image, but the report format should look as shown.

Now that we have successfully downloaded the Geth, let's understand what we can do with it. First, let's synchronize the Blockchain and become a peer in the public testnet network.

Synchronizing the Testnet Blockchain

We have studied that every peer has a copy of the complete chain in a Blockchain network. To become a peer, one must first get a copy of the Blockchain from the other peers in the network. It is called synchronization or sync, and this operation copies the blockchain data from the Genesis block to the recent block.

Here's the command to start the synchronization process:

`./geth --testnet --syncmode "fast"`

Understand the command parameters:

- `--testnet`: This means we need to sync the testnet data only, which is smaller in size than mainnet.
- `--syncmode`: This selects various modes that we can use to sync the chain. In the fast mode, Geth does not validate every block, which reduces the time to sync the chain.

However, syncing the whole chain may take a day depending on your internet connection bandwidth.

You should see the following in the console after running the command:

```
INFO [03-03|17:26:20.221] Allocated fast sync bloom                si
ze=512.00MiB
INFO [03-03|17:26:20.237] New local node record                    se
q=1 id=eaab80f9ccff163b ip=127.0.0.1 udp=30303 tcp=30303
INFO [03-03|17:26:20.238] Started P2P networking                   se
lf=enode://f18bf6ad67a43df003961a436bd97f53c57d50d94e65fe5bdb13fdb4e
41389e0b08407d508b1976fb261a519e98eb6bba161e790b9ae1e0bab0fbcadc1d100
a@127.0.0.1:30303
INFO [03-03|17:26:20.241] IPC endpoint opened                      ur
l=/home/shahidshaikh/.ethereum/testnet/geth.ipc
INFO [03-03|17:26:20.266] Initialized fast sync bloom              it
ems=355 errorrate=0.000 elapsed=44.225ms
WARN [03-03|17:26:21.969] Dropping unsynced node during fast sync  id
=c7e7675577416d6b conn=dyndial addr=52.176.100.77:30303 type=Parity-E
thereum/v2.5.11-stable-fc129b4-20191205/x86_64-linux-gnu/rustc1.39.0
INFO [03-03|17:26:25.704] New local node record                    se
q=2 id=eaab80f9ccff163b ip=114.143.107.254 udp=30303 tcp=30303
```

Figure 2.5

To check sync status, you can check the terminal and find the pending values. Those are the number of blocks that are required to sync before our machine can become a peer in the Ethereum testnet network.

Let's see how to install a private Blockchain software called Ganache that is specially designed for a development purpose.

Installing Ganache

Ganache is a software that allows you to quickly fire up a personal Ethereum blockchain that can be used to run tests and execute smart contracts without becoming a peer.

To download Ganache, visit the official website and download the software form: **https://www.trufflesuite.com/ganache**. Once you have downloaded the software, unzip it and run it in your system.

Ganache looks like this upon running:

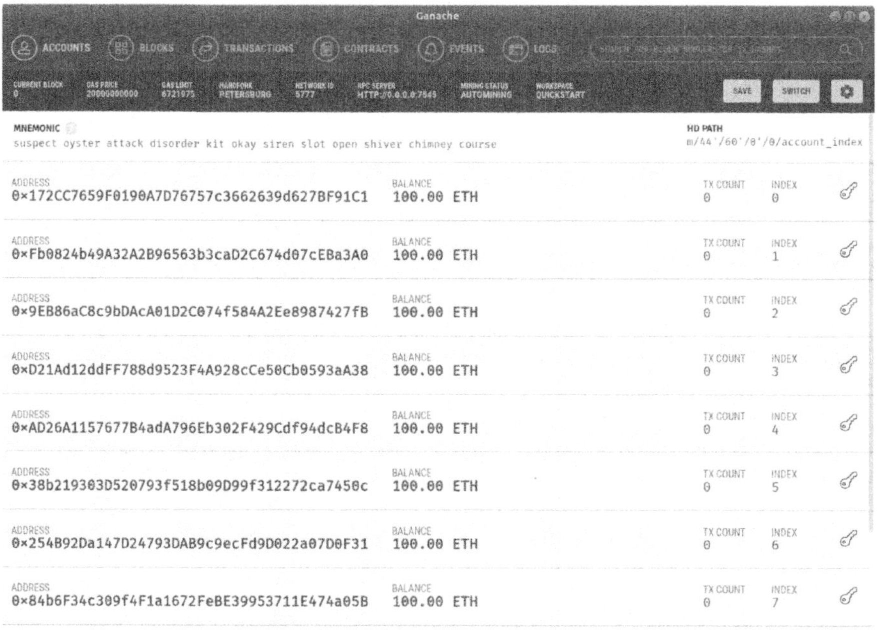

Figure 2.6

Ganache provides multiple test wallets with test Ethers so that you can perform a test. You can check the block and transaction status.

Ganache also has a CLI package that we can install to interact with the Ganache RPC server in a command-line mode.

Let's look at the remote Ethereum client provider and see how we can use it. We will use the `Infura.io` service.

Infura

Infura is a third-party Ethereum and IPFS API provider. You can use Infura infrastructure to run your applications for free. Infura handles all the synchronization and infrastructure hassles, while you, as a developer, can focus on code:

Ethereum, Smart Contracts, and DApps ■ 47

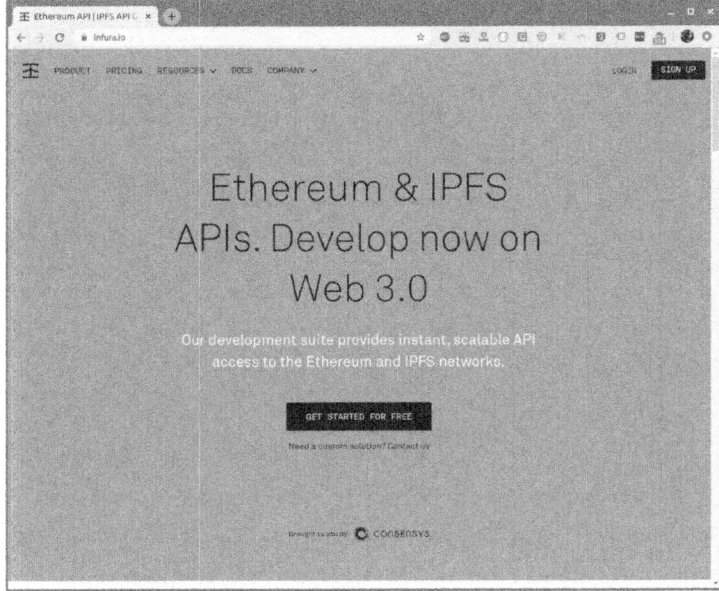

Figure 2.7: *Infura.io Website (Link: https://infura.io/)*

To use Infura service, you need to create your account, for which you can use an email address. Once your account is created, you can log in to the Infura dashboard, which lists the projects you have created with Infura, along with some other details. It looks like this:

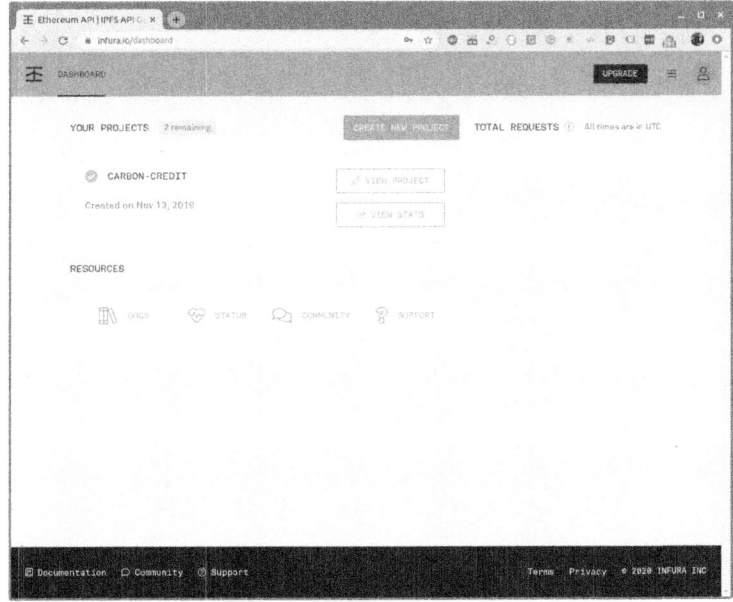

Figure 2.8

As you can see in the preceding image, I have already created a project. You can create your project by clicking on the button called **CREATE NEW PROJECT**. Give your project a proper name, and Infura will create a test and mainnet network for your project behind the scenes.

Once your project is created, you can view all the details such as the peer endpoint that you can use to connect to your peer and project ID and secret.

You can use the credentials to interact with the Infura network. Ensure that it's safe. In the next section, we'll take a brief look at the JSON-RPC API provided by the Ethereum clients.

JSON RPC API

Ethereum clients provide an application programming interface and a set of **Remote Procedure Call (RPC)** commands, which are encoded as **JavaScript Object Notation (JSON).** We refer to this as the JSON-RPC API.

The JSON-RPC API is an interface that allows us to write programs that use an Ethereum client as a gateway to an Ethereum network and Blockchain. We can interact with JSON RPC Server either by building an RPC client in a programming language of your choice, or we can directly call the HTTP endpoint.

First, let's make a simple HTTP call to the Ethereum RPC endpoint and see if it works. Here's the command that will return us the client version:

```
curl -X POST -H "Content-Type: application/json" --data \
  '{"jsonrpc":"2.0","method":"web3_clientVersion","params":[],"id":1}' \
  http://localhost:7545
```

In the preceding command, we are sending the JSON RPC call to the RPC Server running at port 7545 (I am using Ganache).

It should return the following output in the Terminal:

```
{"id":1,"jsonrpc":"2.0","result":"EthereumJS TestRPC/v2.8.0/ethereum-js"}
```

It may vary if you are using Geth or Infura. You can check out all of the commands in the GitHub Wiki of Ethereum: **https://github.com/ethereum/wiki/wiki/JSON-RPC#json-rpc-methods**.

Let's make another RPC call. This time, we will ask the RPC server to return the latest block number.

Here's the command. Copy and paste it in your Terminal:

```
curl -X POST -H "Content-Type: application/json" --data \
   '{"jsonrpc":"2.0","method":"eth_blockNumber","params":[],"id":1}' \
   http://localhost:7545
```

This should return the following output:

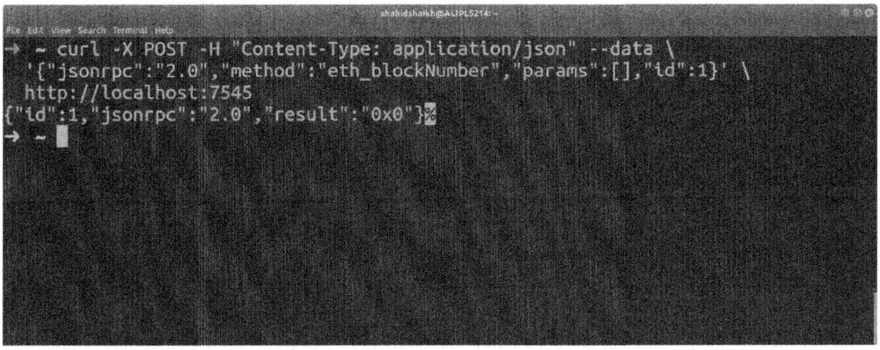

Figure 2.9

You can convert the 0x0 that is hexadecimal into a decimal by running the following command in the Terminal:
```
$ echo $((0x0))
$ 0
```

You should try other commands and interact with the RPC to gain the command over the functions and methods of Ethereum chain. We will use these functions in the upcoming section to program our smart contracts.

Till now, we studied Ethereum in detail and learned how to become a peer in the Ethereum network; we also looked at the Ethereum RPC calls and how to use and interact with it.

In the next section, we will learn about Smart contracts and Solidity programming language.

Smart Contracts and Solidity Language

Smart contracts are programs that run on Ethereum Virtual Machines or EVMs and govern the behavior of accounts in the Ethereum state.

Let's understand this definition:

- **Computer programs:** Smart contracts are simply computer programs like any other program. The word "contract" has no legal meaning per say.
- **Immutable:** Once a smart contract is deployed, it can be changed to meet the basic criteria of Blockchain, that is, immutability. A new change has to be deployed again with a new version number.
- **Virtual machine context:** Smart contracts run under a limited execution context. Smart contracts can access their state, the context of the transaction, and information about the most recent blocks if required.
- **Decentralized computer:** Virtual machines run on each node around the world and share the same state, so the whole system operates as a single computer.

Smart contracts are widely written in the Solidity programming language.

"Solidity is an object-oriented, high-level programming language for implementing smart contract programs for Ethereum."

Solidity is heavily inspired by the C++, Python, and JavaScript, and you will find it familiar if you have worked on any of these programming languages in your career. Solidity is statically typed (that means types are checked during compile time), and it supports inheritance, libraries, and user-defined types.

In this section, we will learn about solidity projects and data types, and we will also develop a program in solidity.

Solidity is a high-level programming language, but it converts its code into machine-level executable code with the help of solidity compilers, which are commonly referred to as solc.

You can install a solidity compiler in your computer in many ways. The simplest way to install the compiler is by using the node package manager, that is, **npm**.

Assuming that you have Node.js installed in your machine, you can run this command in the terminal to install a solidity compiler:

```
sudo npm install -g solc
```

This command will install a solidity compiler in your machine. Once the installation is complete, you can verify it by running the following command:

```
$ solcjs -h
```

This command will print the options related to solidity compilers, as illustrated in the following screenshot:

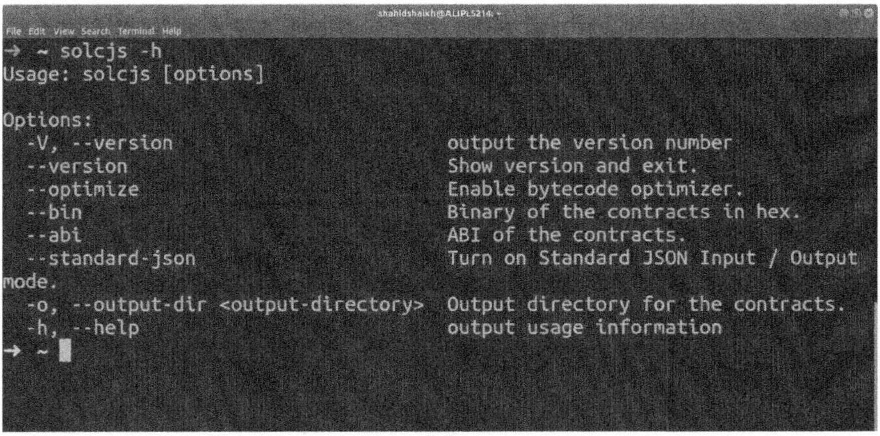

Figure 2.10

You can visit the official website of solidity for detailed installation instructions: **https://solidity.readthedocs.io/en/latest/installing-solidity.html**.

Let's look over the data types of Solidity programming language. We can cover every detail about Solidity in one section, but I will try to explain the must-know stuff to help you start writing Solidity programs or smart contracts.

Solidity Data Types

Look over some of the basic data types of Solidity:

- **Boolean:** Boolean value; holds `true` or `false`.

- **Integer:** Signed integer (int) and unsigned integer (uint) are declared as a 256-bit integer value. However, we can provide the size suffix in increments of 8. For example, int8, int16 to uint256.
- **Fixed point:** Fixed-point numbers, declared with fixedMxN or ufixedMxN, where M is the size of bits in the increment of 8 and N is the number of decimals after the point. For example, ufixed32x2 means unsigned fixed point with 32 bit in size and two decimal points.
- **Address:** It's a 20-byte Ethereum address type. Address payable is a type that provides additional members to transfer and send, and it is the address where one can send ethers.
- **Arrays:** It comes in two types:
   a) Fixed types are fixed-size arrays declared with bytes1 and bytes32.
   b) Dynamic arrays vary in size. They are declared with bytes or string.
- **Enum:** It's a user-defined type for discrete values.
- **Struct:** It's a user-defined data container similar to structures in C++.
- **Mapping:** It's a hash lookup table by mapping keys with values.

These are basic types to handle data. There are also time and ether units that follow standard units. Time converts to milliseconds and Ether to the wei base unit.

Note: wei is the smallest unit of the **Ether**.

Let's look over the structure of a contract to understand how to write contracts.

Contract Structure

Each contract, in solidity, can contain the following:
- State variables
- Functions
- Function modifier
- Events
- Struct and Enum types

Contracts can also inherit other well-written contracts for code reusability. Let's understand the contract structure in detail.

State Variables

State variables are variables whose values are permanently stored in the contract. Any variable declared with the types we learned earlier are state variables, and it is permanently restored.

Consider this example:

```
pragma solidity 0.4.0;
contract SimpleStorage {
    uint storedData; // State variable
    // ...
}
```

Functions

Functions contain code and can be invoked by calling them from the program. Functions have visibility such as public, private, and so on. They accept parameters and return variables.

Refer to this example:

```
pragma solidity >=0.4.0 <0.7.0;

contract SimpleAuction {
function sayHello() public payable { // Function
        // ...
    }
}
```

Function Modifier

Function modifiers can be used to change the behavior of functions in a declarative way. For example, we can use a modifier to execute a conditional code before executing functions.

Events

As the name suggests, it provides functionality to emit and subscribe to events. Events allow programmers to write modular and clean codebase.

Struct

Struct—short for Structure—is the way to define a user-generated data structure.

Take a look at this example:

```
pragma solidity 0.4.0;

contract UserInfo {
    struct User { // Struct
        uint Id;
byte32 name;
address delegate;
    }
}
```

Enum

Enum data types allow developers to create their type in Solidity.

Consider this example:

```
pragma solidity 0.4.0;

contract Purchase {
enumUserStatus { Active, Pending, Inactive } // Enum
}
```

Let's write our first Solidity program, and I will clear all doubts you might have by going through the preceding example code.

Writing Our First Solidity Program

Let's write our first smart contract. You must have the following things installed in your machine:

- NodeJS
- Truffle
- Solc - Solidity compiler
- Ganache either GUI or command line

You can choose the code editor of your choice, but I would highly recommend you to use VSCode or Visual Studio code editor.

You can download the editor from the official website. Here is the link VSCode official link: **https://code.visualstudio.com/**

If you are using VSCode, I recommend you to install the Solidity extension. Let's start:

1. To install, click on the Extension icon in the VSCode left bar and search for solidity.
2. Click on the **Install** button, and you are good to go.
3. Assuming that you have Node and Ganache installed as we played around with them in the previous section, let me show you how to install truffle.

Truffle is an Ethereum development framework suit, and it makes writing smart contracts easy:

1. Run this command to install Truffle in your machine:
   ```
   $ sudo npm install -g truffle
   ```
2. Once it is installed, we can move ahead with the project.
3. Create a new folder and navigate to it using the command line. Run this command to create a new Solidity project.
4. To create a folder:
   ```
   $ mkdir solidityDemo
   $ cd solidityDemo
   ```
5. Then, run the following command:
   ```
   $ truffle init
   ```

It should provide the following output in the Terminal:

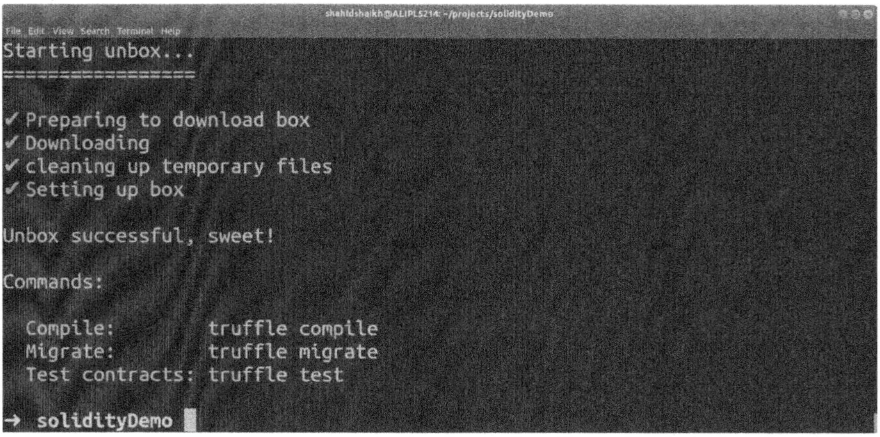

Figure 2.11

Awesome!

Now, open the project in your code editor. Here is the structure of the project:

contracts

migrations

test

truffle-config.js

The Contracts folder stores the code written in Solidity. The Migrations folders contain the deployed contracts. Truffle-config.js contains configuration documents; we don't need to touch that file for our project.

1. Create a new file in the contracts folder and name it hello.sol. Copy paste the following code into it:

   ```
   pragma solidity ^0.5.16;

   contract HelloWorld {
   function hi() public pure returns (string memory) {
   return ("Hello World");
       }
   }
   ```

Let's understand the program before moving ahead.
1. The first line tells the compiler which version of solidity to use. It is important. Change the version of solc to your version if it is different from 0.5.16, as shown above.
2. The second line creates a new contract, where we create a new function that returns a string saying *"Hello World"*.
3. Let's compile this program by running this command:

    $ truffle compile

    It should return the following output in the console:

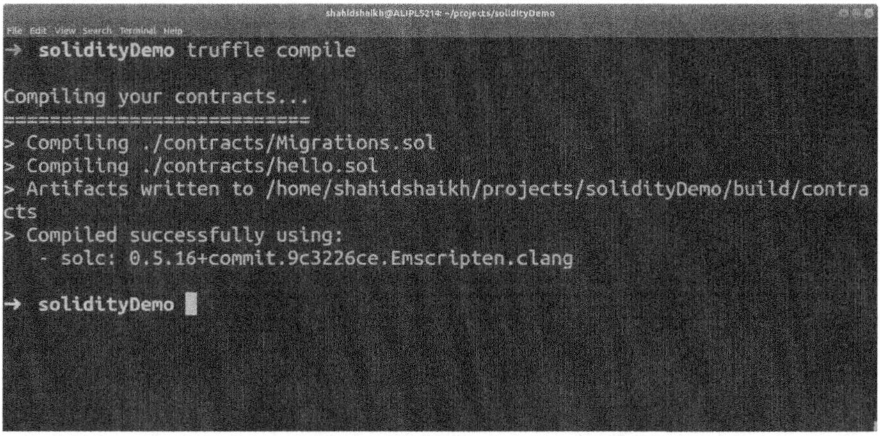

Figure 2.12

4. Now, let's deploy the contract. In the migrations folder, create a new file named 2_deploy_contracts.js and copy paste the following code:

    constHelloWorld = artifacts.require ("HelloWorld");

    module.exports = function(deployer) {

    deployer.deploy(HelloWorld);

    }

    In the first line, we are loading our contract by name and then deploying it using the global deployer object.

5. Now, open the truffle-config.js file and change the uncomment or add the following in the networks object:

    development: {

    host: "127.0.0.1",   // Localhost (default: none)

    port: 7545,   // Standard Ethereum port

```
(default: none)
network_id: "*",        // Any network (default: none)
},
```

This configuration will point towards the Ganache blockchain. You can change it according to your system.

6. Let's deploy our contract to our Blockchain. Run the following command:

$ truffle deploy

It will deploy our smart contract in Blockchain and return the transaction ID. This command should print something like this at your end:

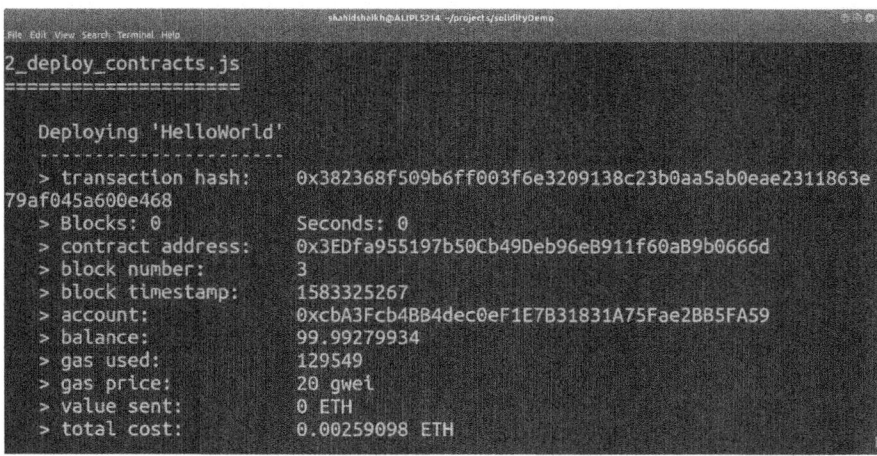

Figure 2.13

7. We can use the transaction hash to view our contract in the Ganache. Just copy the transaction hash and paste it in search of the Ganache:

Figure 2.14

Congratulations! You have successfully created, compiled, and deployed a smart contract in Ethereum blockchain.

We have covered Solidity in brief in this section; you can learn more about it in the official documentation. It's an interesting language and will help you gain experience in the static type language with state management.

In the next section, we will learn about the decentralized apps framework by Ethereum.

Decentralized Apps (DApps) Using Ethereum

In this section, we will explore decentralized application development using the Ethereum platform. A decentralized application built with Ethereum is an application that executes smart contracts in the backend and hosts frontend in the decentralized network.

In a nutshell, a decentralized application using Ethereum is composed of the following:

- **Front end:** HTML, CSS, JavaScript, and static files
- **Backend:** Smart contracts, Blockchain

An application may require more than just smart contracts, and Ethereum provides the following projects to cover these needs:
- **Swarm:** Decentralized storage network
- **Whisper:** Dynamic communication protocol
- **Smart contracts:** Turing complete programming language and interface

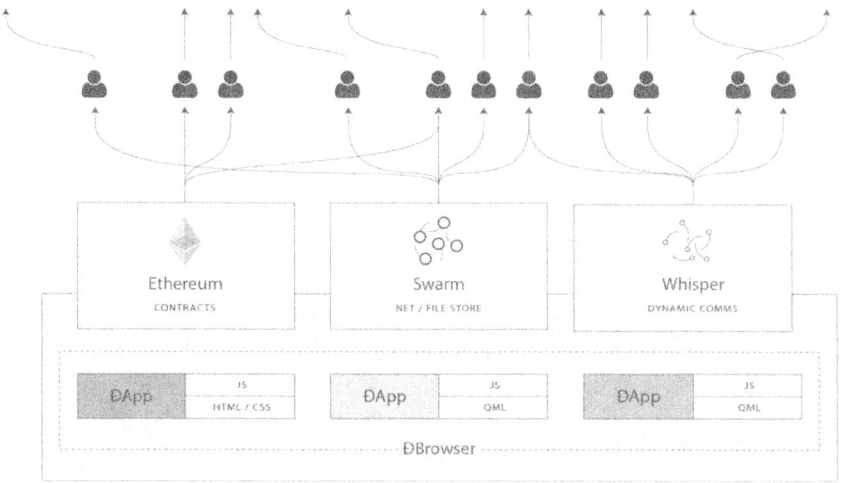

Figure 2.15: Decentralized Web Stack by Ethereum

Consider the following aspect of an application that may be decentralized:
- Frontend
- Backend
- Storage
- Communication
- Name resolution

Each of these aspects can be somewhat centralized or decentralized. For example, frontend can run as an independent centralized server, while backend is a smart contract running on Blockchain. Storage can be used as decentralized, while name resolution can be a centralized service.

At this moment, there is no hard and fast rule that all aspects of the application have to be decentralized. You must use Blockchain, of course, to put business logic in check with decentralization; the rest can mix up with centralized service to improve user experience. Again, it's not necessary either.

Let's check out the advantages of the decentralized applications:

- **Resiliency:** Business logic of the app is written in the smart contract, which, in turn, executes in Blockchain. Unlike an application deployed on a centralized server, a DApp will have no downtime due to the network strength.
- **Transparency:** Any interaction with DApp is stored in the Blockchain. Anyone can check that in the chain and be sure about the code. DApp code, execution, and result are completely transparent with zero censorship.
- **Censorship resistance:** As long as the network is up, anyone can access and use the application running on the chain. There is no stopping, censorship, and permission required to access the application. It is necessary right now when everything in the tech world is getting censored.
- **Trustless system:** Unlike in centralized applications where users trust companies to store their data in the safest possible way, everything is end-to-end cryptographically secure in decentralized applications.
- **Security:** Due to the use of end-to-end cryptography, decentralized applications are secure and solid. Nothing can be accessed except by human error, as machines and networks don't leak any data.
- **No Single point of failure:** Due to the decentralized nature of the application, there is no single point of failure present in the system. Unless there is a node in the network alive, the application will work.
- **Payment:** Since DApps runs on top of the Ethereum blockchain, there is no need to perform third-party payment integration. Payment is facilitated in the crypto coins and recorded in the chain.

As you can see, decentralized application points to some of the core issues that we are facing right now. Censorship, financial frauds, documents' tampering, and elections' rigging are some of the common things we hear right now. Decentralized applications and Blockchain address these issues and help us evolve to the next version of the Web, that is, Web3.0 - Internet by the people, for the people.

Let's take a look at the development stack of decentralized applications.

DApps Stack

The DApps stack in Ethereum comprises the following:
- Front-end (HTML, CSS, JavaScript)
- Smart contracts
- Data storage - IPFS and Swarm
- Decentralized Message Communication - Whisper

Let's understand them in detail.

Front-end

The front-end of decentralized applications can be written in the standard technologies that have been used over the decades to build websites and apps.

Unlike the backend, where one needs to understand how Ethereum works and write code in Solidity, the front-end can be written in HTML, CSS, and JavaScript, which are widely used to build web apps.

This allows traditional web developers to use familiar technologies and tools, frameworks, and libraries. The communication to Blockchain can be carried out via API or RPC calls.

Ethereum also developed a JavaScript library called web3.js, which is used to bundle the front-end with the backend of the DApp.

Web3.js provides an easy and familiar way for traditional web developers to build decentralized apps that can communicate with the Blockchain via the browser.

Let's look over the backend, that is, smart contracts stack.

Smart Contracts (Backend of the App)

In DApps, smart contracts are used to write the business logic and related functions of your application. You can think of a smart contract replacing a server-side (aka "backend") layer in a traditional application.

Developers must keep in mind that any computation executed in a smart contract is expensive in terms of ethers and should be kept to a mininum. So, it is important to identify the aspects of the application that need to run on a decentralized platform.

Smart contracts let you build applications in which a network of smart contracts call and pass data between each other, reading and writing their state variables as they go.

A major point to note in the smart contract architecture design is the inability to change the code of a contract once it is deployed.

A smart contract can be deleted if it is programmed with an available SELFDESTRUCT opcode, but other than that, the code cannot be changed in any way.

Another major point to note is that the size of DApps should be as light as possible. A really large smart contract may cost way too much gas (ethers) to execute, making it inefficient.

As a developer, you should only keep business logic in the smart contract. Storage can be either dealt with centralized services or using Swarm or IPFS.

Let's look over the storage stack and understand how to keep the storage part away from the smart contract so that we avoid building a very large contract that costs a fortune to run in the Blockchain.

Storage

Due to high costs to execute contracts, smart contracts are not a good option for storing or processing large amounts of data such as photos, videos, and so on.

So, DApps should utilize off-chain data storage services, meaning they store the bulky data of the Ethereum chain on a data storage platform.

The data storage platform can be centralized (for example, a typical cloud database like Amazon or Azure), or the data can be decentralized, stored on a peer-to-peer network such as the IPFS or Ethereum's own Swarm platform.

Decentralized peer-to-peer network storage is ideal for storing and distributing large assets such as images, videos, and static resources such as normal files.

Let's look over the options we have at the time of writing this book to use as decentralized P2P storage.

IPFS

IPFS or the **Interplanetary File System** is a decentralized peer-to-peer network to store and share content. IPFS is a project by the protocol labs team and uses content addressing; so, a unique hash identifies each file added in the network. You can retrieve the file using the hash from any node in the network.

IPFS aims to replace the HTTP protocol for standard content delivery for the Web. IPFS has a network, and anyone can become a part of it, just like in Bitcoin or Ethereum.

In the next chapter, we will learn about IPFS in depth. Let's check our next decentralized P2P network storage.

Swarm

Swarm is a project by Ethereum foundation. It is a content-addressable P2P storage system very similar to IPFS, and it allows you to host and access a website using the network.

Let's run a simple Swarm instance and check it for ourselves.

You can download Swarm from the official website for your desired operating system

Link: **https://ethersphere.github.io/swarm-home/downloads/**

Once you have downloaded it, you can unzip the file and run swarm from the Terminal:

```
$ ./swarm
```

Once the Swarm is running, you can visit the Swarm gateway from the browser by navigating to `localhost:8500`.

You should see a screen similar to this:

Figure 2.16

Now, let's check out the working of the Swarm:

First, upload a file either from the browser by going to the upload tab or via command line.

Here's the command:

```
$ ./swarm up <path of the file>
```

It will return the hash of the file. Check out the following image as a reference:

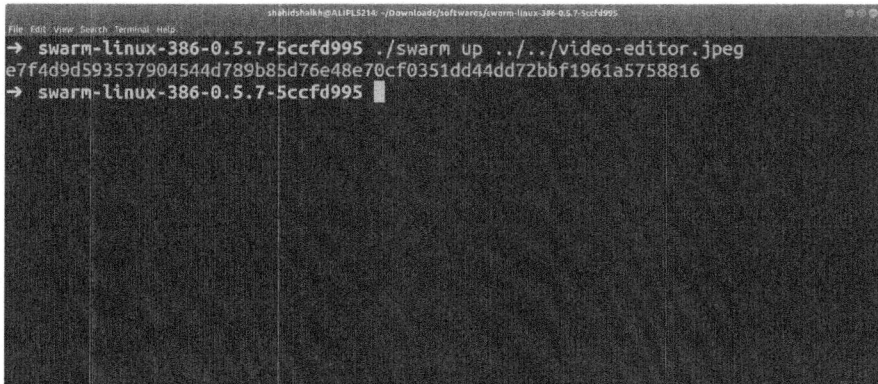

Figure 2.17

Now, copy the hash and navigate to the following URL:

`localhost:8500/bzz:/<your hash>`

It should retrieve the content and show it to the browser.

Awesome, isn't it? How easy it is just to download some software and become a part of a decentralized network.

Alright, let's visit our last part in the DApps stack.

Decentralized Message Communications Protocols

One of the crucial components in any distributed applications is inter-process communication. The application must be able to communicate with other instances via some medium to exchange data back and forth while maintaining the state.

In conventional applications, message queues and inter-process channels were the way to handle such communications. These message queues are central in nature and introduce another single point of failure in the system.

In decentralized applications, communication is done via the P2P messaging protocol. At the time of writing this book, the most notable and widely accepted communication protocol for DApps is the Whisper by Ethereum foundation.

Ethereum also provides a service called Ethereum Name Service or ENS. Developers can use ENS to point the hash-based resources to more friendly human-readable names similar to how we do in DNS services.

Conclusion

In this chapter, we dived deeper into Ethereum. We studied the vision and platform and how one can use Ethereum. We also studied various parts of Ethereum, such as EVM and smart contracts, and we built a simple application to see how smart contracts work. We looked at building decentralized applications using Ethereum, and we explored the various protocols that are required to build a decentralized application.

In the next chapter, we will learn about IPFS in depth. We will build an application that uses IPFS and deploy it to see how it works in real-time.

CHAPTER 3
Interplanetary File System

An **Interplanetary File System (IPFS)** is a distributed system to store, access, and share files. IPFS has an ambitious goal to turn the existing centralized Internet to distributed Internet. It aims to replace HTTP as a default protocol to share files over the Internet.

Structure

In this chapter, we will learn the following:
- Introduction to IPFS
- How IPFS works
- Installing and configuring IPFS
- Hosting static website using IPFS
- Building a full-stack app using IPFS in the backend
- IPFS cluster

Objective

After studying this chapter, you should be able to:
- Understand IPFS and its working

- Understand the core concepts of IPFS
- Use IPFS to build the application

Let's get started.

Introduction to IPFS

According to the IPFS official website:

IPFS is a distributed system for storing and accessing files, websites, applications, and data.

IPFS provides a platform for developers to store data on distributed platforms. There are projects such as **OrbitDB** (we will learn about it in the upcoming chapters) that provide database solutions on top of IPFS. Due to the distributed nature of IPFS, it's the first choice for decentralized application development. In the previous chapter, we studied building applications using Ethereum and used Swarm as a storage solution. IPFS uses content-based addressing instead of location-based addressing to access files. So, location-based addressing is what we will use; currently, we use domain names or IP addresses to access the content.

Consider this example:

https://abc.com/hello.html

Here, we are accessing the hello.html file using the domain name. The domain name, in turn, looks out for the IP address of the server and picks up the file from the server.

In the IPFS, we use content-addressing. Let's look at an example:

https://ipfs.io/QmXoypizjW3WknFiJnKLwHCnL72vedxjQkDDP1mXWo6uco/hello.html

As you can see here, we access the content by the hash. Hash represents the file and not the location where the file is stored. It's the responsibility of the IPFS network to collect the bits and pieces of the file and deliver them to the user.

Let's understand how IPFS works.

How IPFS works

IPFS is a distributed peer-to-peer storage network. In IPFS, content is accessed from peers spread across the world. Peers in IPFS can relay information, store information, or do both.

IPFS works by forming a network using independent peers. These peers store and relay files information asked by the users.

IPFS uses the following important modules to make the network work:

- Content-based addressing
- Direct acyclic graph
- Distributed hash table

Let's explore these modules in detail.

Content-based Addressing

IPFS uses content-based addressing to identify data by what's in it, rather than by where it's located.

Looking for an item by content is something we already do. For example, when you look for a piece of cloth, you often ask for it by the color or type; that's content addressing because you're asking for what it is.

If you were using location addressing to find that cloth, you'd ask for it by where it is: *"I want the t-shirt that's on the second rack, three pieces of cloth away from the left."* If someone moved that cloth, you'd be out of luck!

This is how we access content on the Internet. For example,

- /Users/Alice/Documents/project_paper.doc
- C:/Users/Joe/My/Documents/presentation.ppt

IPFS, in turn, generates the Content Identifier (CID), which is also referred to as the hash.

Content addressing by using a hash is widely used to connect data in distributed systems. You can see the hash-based content addressed in the Git to the cryptocurrencies. It's everywhere.

However, the underlying data structures in these systems are not always interoperable. Every system uses a different set of data sets and structures. To tackle such issues, IPFS developed **Interplanetary Linked Data (IPLD),** which acts as a data model for content addressing. IPLD acts as a translation layer between different types of data sets used by the different systems. So, IPFS uses content-addressing using the hash, and IPLD performs the data sets' translation, if required, to enable smooth transition of data from one system to another.

Let's look at the next module.

Direct Acyclic Graph

IPFS uses a **Direct Acyclic Graph(DAG)** to store the content. It uses Merkle DAG, which is hashing together leaf nodes to form a parent node. We studied the Merkle tree in the first chapter.

DAG is a graph in which edges have direction and cycles are not allowed.

For example, a linked list like A—›B—›C is an instance of a DAG where A references B, and so on. We say that B is a child or a descendant of A, and node A has a link to B. Similarly, A is a parent of B.

In DAG, nodes that are not children to any other node are referred to as root nodes.

A Merkle-DAG is a DAG where each node has an identifier (hash or CID), and this is the result of hashing the node's contents with the SHA256 function. Merkle-DAG node is immutable. Any change in the node, in turn, creates a different Merkle-DAG.

IPFS builds the Merkle-DAG tree of the content by splitting the content into blocks. Each of these blocks is then associated with CID and then hashed together from the leaf node to form a Merkle-DAG tree.

So, IPFS provides content-based addressing using hash and Merkle-DAG links, which hash together to form content. Let's learn about the next and last module—Distributed Hash Table or DHT.

Distributed Hash Table

A hash table is a set of key-value pairs, and a distributed hash table is where the table is distributed across the different peers in the network.

The main advantages of DHTs are decentralization, fault tolerance, and scalability. Due to this, the hash table can span across millions of nodes, and data availability is higher due to the distributed nature of data.

IPFS has a separate library called libp2p, which deals with distributed hash tables and peer networking.

IPFS uses DHT to find the current location of the content and peers. Once the content is found, IPFS connects to the content and downloads it to your system. Once these blocks are downloaded, you can calculate the hash and verify the authenticity of the content.

Libp2p also handles peer-to-peer networking and connection multiplexing. Connection multiplexing allows Libp2p to use a single connection for multiple services.

We will learn more about DHT in the coming section. Now, let's install IPFS in our system.

Installing and Configuring IPFS

Let's install IPFS in our system and become a peer:

1. Navigate to the official IPFS website at **https://dist.ipfs.io/#go-ipfs** and download the IPFS package for your system. As shown in the following image, select your operating system to download the correct version of IPFS:

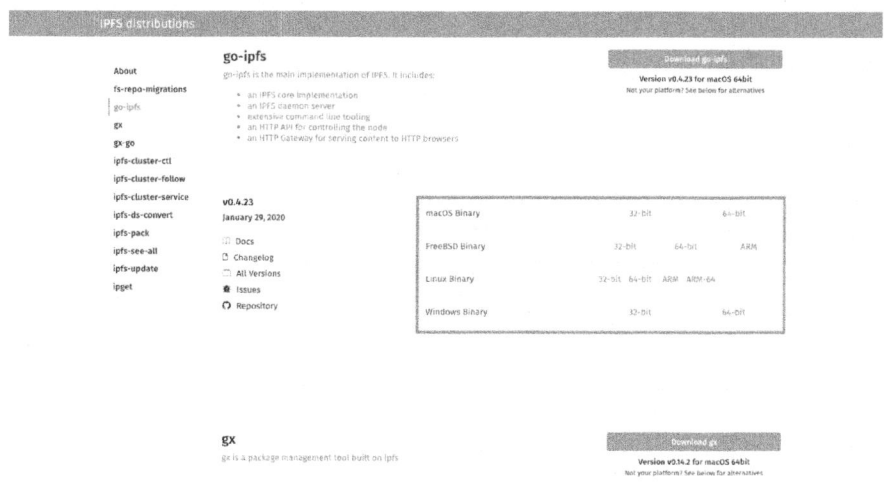

Figure 3.1

2. Once you have downloaded the package, extract or unzip it and switch to the extracted folder. This command installs the IPFS in your system.

   ```
   cd go-ipfs
   ./install.sh
   ```

72 ■ *Building Decentralized Blockchain Applications*

3. Once IPFS installed, you can verify it by running the following command:

   `$ ipfs help`

   It should print the IPFS commands in the Terminal, as shown in the following screenshot:

   ```
   ~ ipfs help
   USAGE
     ipfs - Global p2p merkle-dag filesystem.

     ipfs [--config=<config> | -c] [--debug=<debug> | -D] [--help=<help>] [-h=<h>]
     [--local=<local> | -L] [--api=<api>] <command> ...

   SUBCOMMANDS
     BASIC COMMANDS
       init                  Initialize ipfs local configuration
       add <path>            Add a file to IPFS
       cat <ref>             Show IPFS object data
       get <ref>             Download IPFS objects
       ls <ref>              List links from an object
       refs <ref>            List hashes of links from an object

     DATA STRUCTURE COMMANDS
       block                 Interact with raw blocks in the datastore
       object                Interact with raw dag nodes
       files                 Interact with objects as if they were a unix filesystem
       dag                   Interact with IPLD documents (experimental)

     ADVANCED COMMANDS
       daemon                Start a long-running daemon process
       mount                 Mount an IPFS read-only mountpoint
       resolve               Resolve any type of name
       name                  Publish and resolve IPNS names
       key                   Create and list IPNS name keypairs
       dns                   Resolve DNS links
       pin                   Pin objects to local storage
       repo                  Manipulate the IPFS repository
       stats                 Various operational stats
   ```

   Figure 3.2

   Now, let's run IPFS in our system:

4. Run this command on your Terminal:

   `$ ipfs init`

   It will initialize the repository and create the required files in your system to run the IPFS.

5. Start the IPFS daemon. To do so, run this command:

   `$ ipfs daemon`

This command will start the IPFS in a daemon (background process) mode. You should see the message in your Terminal, as follows:

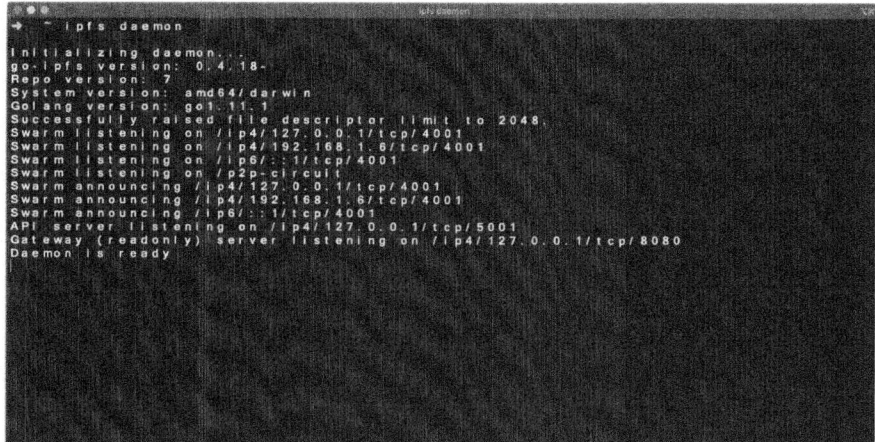

Figure 3.3

6. Now, navigate to **http://localhost:5001/webui**; you should see the admin screen, as follows:

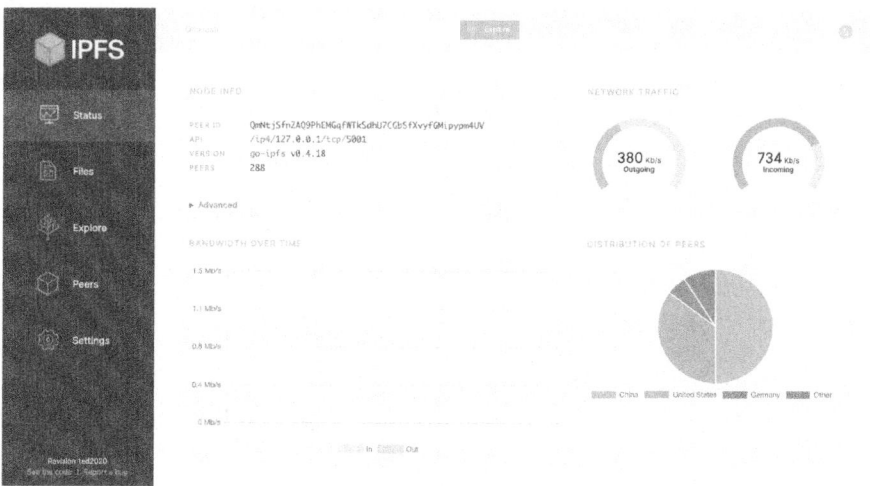

Figure 3.4

In the admin screen, you can see the node information, such as Peer ID, IPFS version, network traffic charts, and peer distribution.

Now, visit the *Peers* page; you should be able to see the peer distribution across the world. It should look like the following screenshot, but the peer's number may vary:

Figure 3.5

Pretty awesome, right? You can see the peers and their IDs scattered across the world. Now you're also a peer, and you can access any documents you like (only if you have the CID or hash of the file).

Let's quickly add a file and try to access it using the IPFS commands.

Run this command to add a file in the IPFS network:

$ ipfs add <path of the file>

This command will generate the hash of the content on the screen if executed successfully:

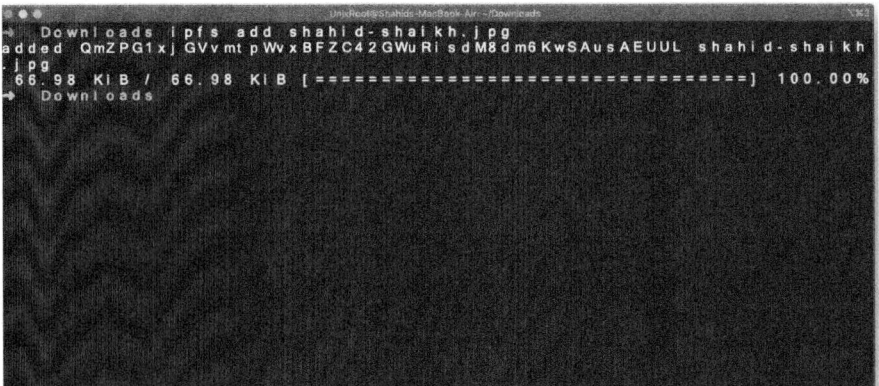

Figure 3.6

Now, copy the hash and access it using the browser:

`localhost:8080/ipfs/<hash of the file>`

You should see the file in your browser, like this:

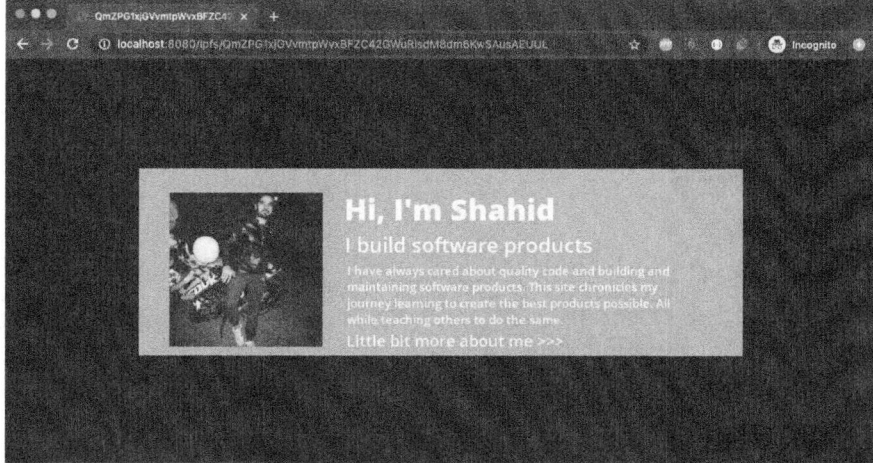

Figure 3.7

You can also access it from anywhere using the global IPFS gateway. Visit the following URL:

https://ipfs.io/ipfs/QmZPG1xjGVvmtpWvxBFZC42GWuRisdM8dm6KwSAusAEUUL

You can replace the hash with your file hash and share it with anyone in the world. You don't need to become a peer to access the file hosted on IPFS.

You can use the following command to access or download the file from the command line:

`$ ipfs get <hash of the file>`

After execution of this command, you should be able to view the downloaded file in the file system.

We will learn more about the command line of IPFS in the next section.

IPFS Command Line

IPFS provides command-line utility for developers to perform IPFS action using command prompt or Terminal.

To check the list of available IPFS commands, run this in your Terminal:

```
$ ipfs --h
```

It will print all the available commands in your Terminal screen, like this:

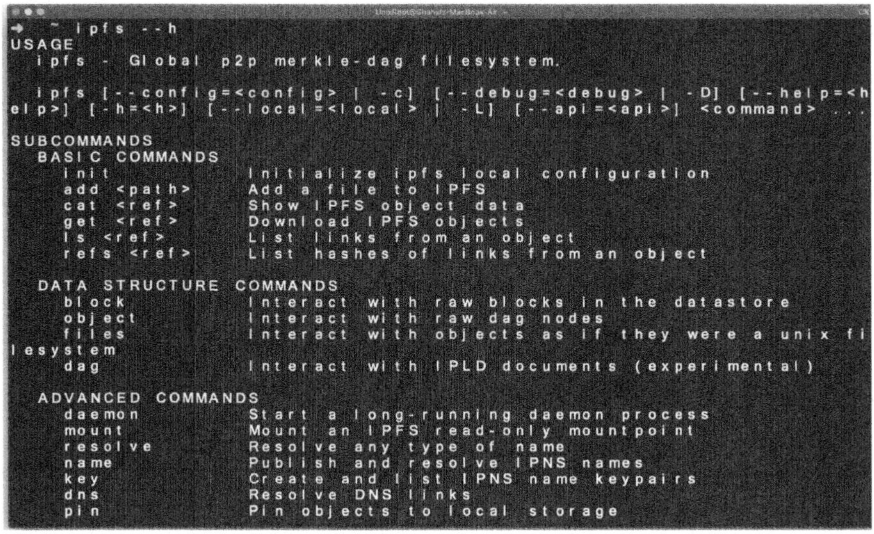

Figure 3.8

There are two types of IPFS commands:
1. **Offline:** These commands can be executed without running an IPFS instance.
2. **Online:** These commands require an IPFS node running in your system.

You can check all the command details on the IPFS official website: **https://docs.ipfs.io/reference/api/cli/**

Now, let's learn how to configure IPFS running in your system or in a cloud server to meet your application requirements.

Configuring IPFS Node

IPFS stores the configuration in a file located at the home folder location of any operating system. The configuration is stored as a **JavaScript Object Notation (JSON)** file. You can view the file at `~/.ipfs/config`.

Open the file in your editor to view the contents. Let's understand the key aspects of the configuration.

Addresses

These are the default addresses on which IPFS is running and should look like this:

```
"Addresses": {
  "API": "/ip4/127.0.0.1/tcp/5001",
  "Announce": [],
  "Gateway": "/ip4/127.0.0.1/tcp/8080",
  "NoAnnounce": [],
  "Swarm": [
    "/ip4/0.0.0.0/tcp/4001",
    "/ip6/::/tcp/4001"
  ]
}
```

You can configure API, gateway addresses. Generally, it is set up to a local host address that can be changed to the custom IP address required. Swarm addresses are addresses where local IPFS nodes will listen to connect to other IPFS nodes. API address is where IPFS exposes its API endpoint so that developers can interact with it.

Gateway is the optional address that can be used to view and host static files. You can make this address public if you want others to store files in your IPFS node. Leave it blank if you don't want Gateway to boot.

Bootstrap

It is a list of addresses in an array that IPFS node connects to after startup. IPFS comes with default bootstrap addresses that you can alter. It is suggested otherwise because IPFS, as an organization, maintains various servers to provide a constant bootstrap connection to new peers.

There are other configuration parameters as well, but it's good to leave it default.

Let's host a website in the IPFS and see how it works.

Hosting a Static Website in IPFS

IPFS is a distributed file system, so we can host a static website directly into the peer-to-peer network of IPFS.

In this section, we will create a website and then host it in the IPFS network. Let's create a simple website.

Our website will look like the following screenshot:

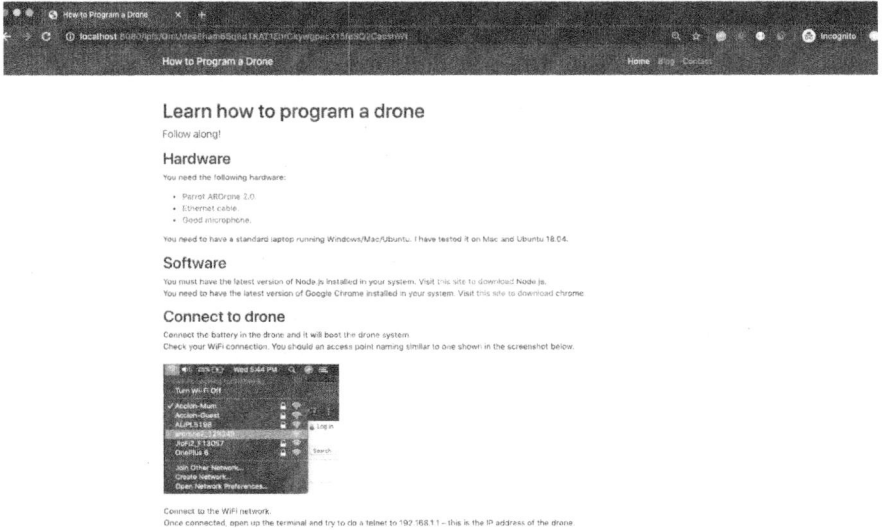

Figure 3.9

You can visit the website using the global IPFS network gateway. Here's the URL:

http://ipfs.io/ipfs/QmUdeaEham65q8dTRAT1EhrCkywgpacX15feSQ2CacshWt

Let's check the code of the website. This website contains one page and a few images that we will download from remote resources.

You can also include images from the local system itself.

Here's the header of the website HTML:

```
<!DOCTYPE html>
<html lang="en">
<head>
```

```
<meta charset="utf-8">
<meta name="viewport" content="width=device-width, initial-scale=1, shrink-to-fit=no">
<meta name="description" content="Learn how to program a drone using Nodejs.">
<meta name="author" content="ShahidShaikh">
<title>How to Program a Drone</title>
<!-- Bootstrap core CSS -->
<link href="https://stackpath.bootstrapcdn.com/bootstrap/4.3.1/css/bootstrap.min.css" rel="stylesheet">
</head>
```

As you can see, we have added bootstrap as our CSS library to style the content, and we added a few meta tags to handle the view area of the website.

Let's look at the content code of the website:

```
<body>
<!-- Navigation -->
<nav class="navbarnavbar-expand-lgnavbar-dark bg-dark static-top">
<div class="container">
<a class="navbar-brand" href="/">How to Program a Drone</a>
<button class="navbar-toggler" type="button" data-toggle="collapse" data-target="#navbarResponsive" aria-controls="navbarResponsive" aria-expanded="false" aria-label="Toggle navigation">
<span class="navbar-toggler-icon"></span>
</button>
<div class="collapse navbar-collapse" id="navbarResponsive">
<ul class="navbar-nav ml-auto">
<li class="nav-item active">
<a class="nav-link" href="/">Home
<span class="sr-only">(current)</span>
</a>
</li>
```

```
<li class="nav-item">
<a class="nav-link" href="https://codeforgeek.com">Blog</a>
</li>
<li class="nav-item">
<a class="nav-link" href="mailto:shahid@codeforgeek.com">Contact</a>
</li>
</ul>
</div>
</div>
</nav>

<!-- Page Content -->
<div class="container">
<div class="row align-items-center">
<div class="col-lg-12">
<h1 class="mt-5">Learn how to program a drone</h1>
<p class="lead">
        Follow along!
</p>
<h2>Hardware</h2>
<p>
```

You need the following hardware:
```
<ul>
<li>
<a href='https://amzn.to/2TCMcvd'>Parrot ARDrone 2.0.</a>
</li>
<li>
<a href='https://amzn.to/2OvhWBE'>Ethernet cable.</a>
</li>
<li>
<a href='https://amzn.to/2JGka28'>Good microphone.</a>
</li>
</ul>
```

Interplanetary File System

You need to have a standard laptop running Windows/Mac/Ubuntu. I have tested it on Mac and Ubuntu 18.04.
```
</p>
<h2>Software</h2>
<p>
```
You must have the latest version of Node.js installed in your system. Visit `<a href='https://nodejs.org/en/download/'>`this site to download`</a>` Node.js.`<br>`

You need to have the latest version of Google Chrome installed in your system. Visit `<a href="https://www.google.com/chrome/">`this site to download`</a>` chrome.
```
</p>
<h2>Connect to drone</h2>
<p>
```
Connect the battery in the drone and it will boot the drone system. `<br>`

Check your WiFi connection. You should an access point naming similar to one shown in the screenshot below.`<br><br>`

`<img src='https://image.codeforgeek.com/wp-content/uploads/2019/03/Drone-wifi-access-point.png?resize=352%2C264&ssl=1'><br><br>`

Connect to the WiFi network. `<br>`Once connected, open up the terminal and try to do a telnet to 192.168.1.1 – this is the IP address of the drone. `<br><br>`

`<img src="https://image.codeforgeek.com/wp-content/uploads/2019/03/Telnet-drone.png?resize=640%2C259&ssl=1"><br><br>`
```
</p>
<h2>Programming the drone</h2>
<p>
```
Let's code our app. First, create a new folder and switch to it using the terminal. `<br><br>`
```
<code>
mkdir drone && cd drone
</code><br>
```
Create a new Node project using the following command.`<br><br>`

```
<code>
npm init --y
</code><br>
          Let's install the required dependency.<br><br>
<code>
npm install --save ar-drone
</code><br>
          Here is the code. <br><br>
<script src="https://gist.github.com/
codeforgeek/514ee981176e344ea4e871f0407b9fed.js"></script>
</p>
<h2>Running the code</h2>
<p>
          Connect to the drone WiFi and run the code using the following command.
<br><br>
<code>node app.js</code>
and see the drone fly and follow the commands as mentioned in the code.
</p>
<p>
          Here is the small demo.<br>
<style>.embed-container { position: relative; padding-bottom: 56.25%; height: 0; overflow: hidden; max-width: 100%; } .embed-container iframe, .embed-container object, .embed-container embed { position: absolute; top: 0; left: 0; width: 100%; height: 100%; }</style><div class='embed-container'><iframesrc='https://www.youtube.com/embed/97yUXCds3tY' frameborder='0' allowfullscreen></iframe></div>
</p>
</div>
</div>
</div>

<!-- Bootstrap core JavaScript -->
<script src="vendor/jquery/jquery.min.js"></script>
<script src="vendor/bootstrap/js/bootstrap.bundle.min.
```

```
js"></script>

</body>

</html>
```

We have added the jQuery library in the footer of the page to avoid loading the library during initial page load. This trick improves the speed of the website.

The code is a little lengthy, but just go through it and understand the syntaxes. It's basic HTML code with standard tags.

Copy paste and save the code in an index.html file, and place it inside the folder.

Now, open your Terminal, navigate to the folder that contains the code, and run this command to host the website in the IPFS:

```
$ ipfs add -r <folder name>
```

This command will add the file present in the folder in a recursive manner. You should receive multiple hashes in your Terminal, and you need to access the `index.html` file, which is an entry point of the website, as illustrated in the following screenshot:

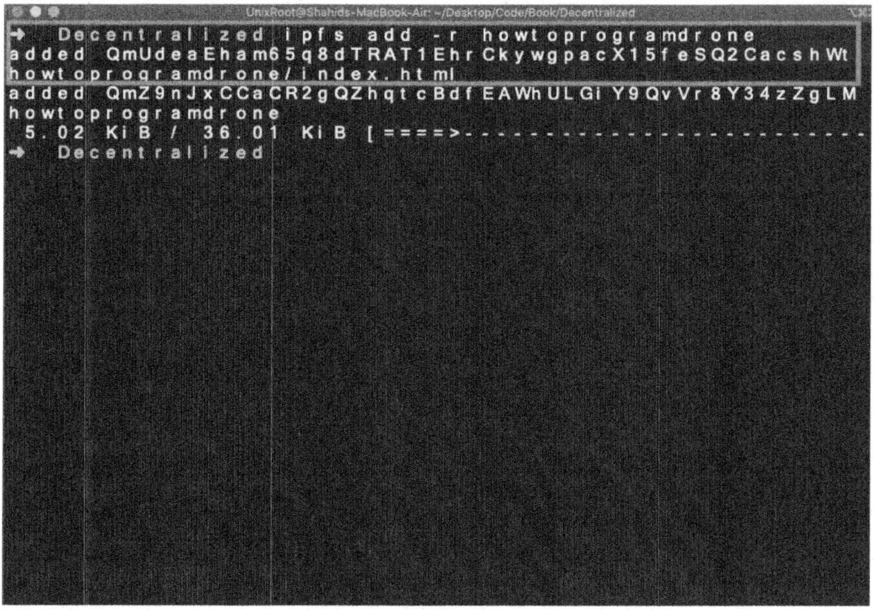
→ Decentralized ipfs add -r howtoprogramdrone
added QmUdeaEham65q8dTRAT1EhrCkywgpacX15feSQ2CacshWt howtoprogramdrone/index.html
added QmZ9nJxCCaCR2gQZhqtcBdfEAWhULGiY9QvVr8Y34zZgLM howtoprogramdrone
5.02 KiB / 36.01 KiB [====>-----------------------
→ Decentralized

Figure 3.10

If you are adding multiple files of the website, you shall receive multiple hashes. To access the website, use the hash of index.html.

This is how you can deploy a static website in the IPFS network. In the next section, we will learn to build and use IPFS in the backend system.

Building a Full-stack App Using IPFS in the Backend

In the last section, we understood how to host a static website in the IPFS network. In this section, we will build an application using IPFS.

We will build a file upload system where the user can upload a file in the IPFS network and get the link to view the uploaded file, just like any other web application uploads files. The only major difference is that we will store the file in the IPFS network.

Here's the technology stack that we will use:
- **Backend:** Node.js framework.
- **Frontend:** HTML, CSS, and jQuery framework
- **Storage:** IPFS network

I am assuming that you have the latest Node.js installed in your system. If not, visit the official Node.js website and get the latest version.

Node.js website: **https://nodejs.org/en/download/**

Let's get going!
1. Create a new directory and navigate to it using the Terminal/command prompt.
2. Create a new Node.js project using the following command:
   `$ npm init --y`
3. Now, let's install the required dependencies that we will use in our project. These dependencies are also called node modules:
   `$ npm install --save express multer ipfs-api`
4. Now, wait for a few seconds and let node install the dependencies. Express is a module that is widely used to build a web application.

Multer is a node module that is used to handle file uploads in the node ecosystem.

`ifps-api` is a node module that is an interface for the IPFS gateway. We will use this module to perform the IPFS operation.

5. Now, create a new file, name it ipfs.js, and copy paste the following code:

```
const IPFS = require('ipfs-api');
const ipfsOptions = {
host: 'localhost',
port: '5001'
};

const ipfs = new IPFS(ipfsOptions);

function addFile(bufferData) {
return new Promise((resolve, reject) => {
ipfs.files.add(bufferData, (err, file) => {
if(err) {
reject(err);
}
resolve(file);
    });
  });
}

module.exports = {
addFile: addFile,
};
```

In the preceding code, we are first connecting to the IPFS that is running on a local machine on 5001 port. You can change it if the port and host details are different in your machine.

We have created a different function to add files to the IPFS network. IPFS takes buffers as an input. We are using the files.add()function provided by the IPFS module to add the file.

The preceding function returns a promise object so that it can be resolved later. It is the best practice to write code in server-side JavaScript.

Next, let's create a server in node. Create a new file called app.js and copy paste the following code:

```
const express = require("express");
const multer = require('multer');
const fs = require('fs');
const app     = express();
const ipfs = require('./ipfs');

const storage = multer.diskStorage({
      destination: function (req, file, callback) {
            callback(null, './uploads');
      },
      filename: function (req, file, callback) {
            callback(null, file.fieldname + '-' + Date.now());
      }
});

const upload = multer({ storage : storage}).single('userPhoto');

app.get('/', (req,res) => {
      res.sendFile(__dirname + "/index.html");
});

app.post('/api/photo', (req,res) => {
      upload(req,res, async (err) => {
      if(err) {
            return res.end("Error uploading file.");
      }
      letfileObject = fs.readFileSync(__dirname + '/' + req.file.path);
      let response = await ipfs.addFile(Buffer.from(fileObject));
      let link = `http://localhost:8080/
```

```
            ipfs/${response[0].hash}`;
            res.end(`File is uploaded - Click <a
            href="${link}">here</a> to view the file`);
      });
});

app.listen(3000,function(){
      console.log("Working on port 3000");
});
```

Let's understand the code.

First, we are requiring the modules in the following code:

```
const express = require("express");
const multer = require('multer');
const fs = require('fs');
const app = express();
const ipfs = require('./ipfs');
```

We also include the code we wrote for the IPFS file upload.

In the next line of code, we are configuring the multer module to upload our files in the local system first:

```
const storage = multer.diskStorage({
      destination: function (req, file, callback) {
            callback(null, './uploads');
      },
            filename: function (req, file, callback) {
                  callback(null, file.fieldname + '-' + Date.now());
      }
});

const upload = multer({ storage : storage}).single('userPhoto');
```

In the preceding code, we have added the uploads directory to store our files. We are also configuring multer to allow the user to upload one file at a time from the userPhoto HTML attribute.

In the next line of code, we are creating a route for our web application. Routes are a way to define the structure of a web application by mapping the URL to the business logic code:

```
app.get('/', (req,res) => {
    res.sendFile(__dirname + "/index.html");
});

app.post('/api/photo', (req,res) => {
    upload(req,res, async (err) => {
    if(err) {
        return res.end("Error uploading file.");
    }
    let fileObject = fs.readFileSync(__dirname + '/' + req.file.path);
    let response = await ipfs.addFile(Buffer.from(fileObject));
    let link = `http://localhost:8080/ipfs/${response[0].hash}`;
    res.end(`File is uploaded - Click <a href="${link}">here</a> to view the file`);
    });
});
```

In the first route, we are delivering the home page to the user. We will look over that code in a moment.

In the next route, we are trying to upload the file in our system. Once the file is uploaded locally, we are reading the file and converting it in the Buffer and then adding it into IPFS using the function we wrote earlier.

Once IPFS returns us the hash of the file, we are returning it to the user in a hyperlink so that the user can view it in the browser.

Note:

Change this line to your custom IPFS host and port if you have made any changes.

```
let link = `http://localhost:8080/ipfs/${response[0].hash}`;
```

Now, let's look at the last piece of HTML code. Create a new file and name it `index.html` and copy paste the following code:

```html
<html>
<head>
<title>File upload using IPFS</title>
</head>
<body>
<h1>File upload system using IPFS</h1>
<form id="uploadForm"
enctype="multipart/form-data"
action="/api/photo"
method="post">
<input type="file" name="userPhoto" />
<input type="submit" value="Upload Image" name="submit"><br />
<span id = "status"></span>
</form>
</body>
<script src="http://ajax.googleapis.com/ajax/libs/jquery/1.7.1/jquery.min.js"></script>
<script src="http://cdnjs.cloudflare.com/ajax/libs/jquery.form/3.51/jquery.form.min.js"></script>
<script>
  $(document).ready(function() {
     $('#uploadForm').submit(function() {
        $("#status").empty().text("File is uploading...");
        $(this).ajaxSubmit({
error: function(xhr) {
status('Error: ' + xhr.status);
        },
success: function(response) {
             $("#status").empty().html(response);
        }
    });
return false;
    });
```

```
});
</script>
</html>
```

In the preceding code, we have included jQuery and jQuery form library from the official CDN.

We have created a form that submits the file data in a multipart format to the API we have created in app.js:

```
<form id="uploadForm"
enctype="multipart/form-data"
action="/api/photo"
method="post">
<input type="file" name="userPhoto" />
```

Notice the action attribute and input name. It must be the same as the API route and multer file section attribute.

In the JavaScript code, we are listening to the response from the server and printing the output. We are also using AJAX to upload files to avoid page refresh.

It's time to run the code. Run the following command in the Terminal/command prompt:

`$ node app.js`

Your Terminal should print a message saying:

`"Working on port 3000"`

It means the app is running successfully. Navigate to `localhost:3000` to view the application. It should look like this:

Figure 3.11

Now, select a file from your system and hit the **Upload Image** button. You should see a response like this:

Figure 3.12

Now, click on the hyperlink to view the image in the IPFS network.

You should see an image you have selected from your system. In my case, it is this. Look at the address bar; it's the IPFS gateway path:

Figure 3.13

Congratulations! You have just built an end-to-end decentralized application using IPFS as a network and storage.

This app uses the latest technologies such as backend system framework—Nodejs—and communicates to the front-end via Ajax.

To deploy this app, you need to deploy the application on a server and connect to the IPFS gateway. You can use the hosted IPFS gateway provided by Infura.io, as discussed in chapter one.

As of now, we have studied about running single IPFS nodes in our machine, but a single IPFS peer is not enough to maintain data redundancy and availability. This is because, well, failure happens. What if one node fails and data is not replicated to another node? It will result in data loss, so not the redundant network. To tackle such a scenario, IPFS introduced the IPFS cluster.

IPFS Cluster

IPFS cluster is a distributed program that runs alongside IPFS peers and allocates and pins data to other peers to maintain data redundancy and availability.

To understand IPFS clusters better, let's look at the architecture diagram provided by the IPFS cluster documentation team:

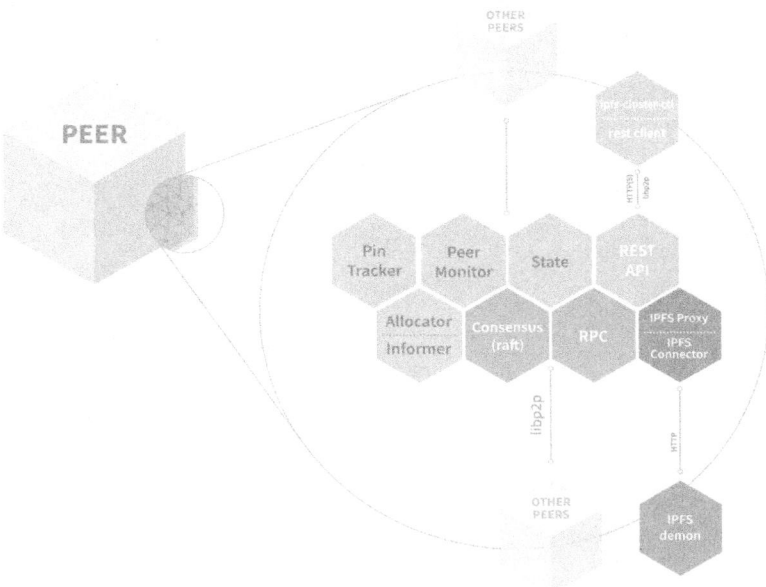

Figure 3.14

As mentioned earlier, the IPFS Cluster program communicates with IPFS peers running in your system. IPFS Cluster communicates using the HTTP API of the IPFS peer, which is running by default on the 5001 port.

IPFS Cluster forms its own network of peers that are running the cluster program and does not interfere with the IPFS network. IPFS cluster peers maintain global data consensus in order to maintain the data redundancy and availability.

You can check out the IPFS cluster official project page to download the program and run it in your system.

IPFS Cluster home page: **https://cluster.ipfs.io/**

One of the core components of the IPFS and IPFS cluster is a module called libp2p. As we studied in chapter one, Libp2p manages peers and provides a framework to build distributed applications.

Since we have already discussed and learned IPFS in detail, it's the perfect time to explore Libp2p in depth and understand the core components of IPFS.

Libp2p

Libp2p is a library, specification, and protocol that helps developers build a peer-to-peer network application.

Libp2p consists of the following components:
- Transport layer protocol
- End-to-end encryption
- Identity module
- Routing
- Content discovery
- Messaging module

Let's discuss these modules in brief.

Transport Layer Protocol

Libp2p transport protocol is the core of the Libp2p. This layer ensures data transmission from one peer to another. The transport layer protocol of Libp2p is evolving every day, and there will be more protocols in the future that will be supported by the Libp2p.

End-to-end Encryption

Libp2p transport layers can be configured to use a secure end-to-end encryption using the latest version of TLS i.e v1.2. TLSv1.3 is under development.

Identity Module

This module ensures that peer is communicating and exchanging data with the correct peer using public-key cryptography to perform an identity check on the data sent and received in the network.

Routing

In the peer-to-peer network, it's essential to have a system to identify and connect to other peers without having to remember the address. Since there is no central system to look for the peer information, Libp2p provides a routing mechanism to ask peers to provide the network address information, and if they don't have it, ask other peers to fetch the same.

Content Discovery

Libp2p allows us to locate content based on the hash and uses the distributed hash table to look up content using the hash or CID.

Messaging Module

In a peer-to-peer network, peer communication is the key. Libp2p provides a publish/subscribe, also called a `pub/sub`, communication module to help peers communicate in real-time.

Libp2p provides software development kits in Java, C++, Go, and JavaScript. Let's build a simple application using server-side JavaScript using *Libp2p*.

We will build a simple application that creates a peer and connects to other peers. We will use the Node.js framework and *js-libp2p*.

Let's create a new node project. Create a new folder and navigate to the folder using command prompt or Terminal:

```
$ npm init --y
```

Let's install the libp2p library and the required dependencies. Run this command in the Terminal:

```
$ npm install --save libp2p libp2p-websockets libp2p-secio
$ npm install --save libp2p-mplex libp2p-bootstrap
```

Once installed, create a new file and name it app.js. Copy paste the following code:

```
const Libp2p = require('libp2p')
const WebSockets = require('libp2p-websockets')
const SECIO = require('libp2p-secio')
const MPLEX = require('libp2p-mplex')
const Bootstrap = require('libp2p-bootstrap')

// peers addresses
const bootstrapMultiaddrs = [
'/dns4/ams-1.bootstrap.libp2p.io/tcp/443/wss/p2p/
QmSoLer265NRgSp2LA3dPaeykiS1J6DifTC88f5uVQKNAd', '/
dns4/lon-1.bootstrap.libp2p.io/tcp/443/wss/p2p/
QmSoLMeWqB7YGVLJN3pNLQpmmEk35v6wYtsMGLzSr5QBU3'
]

async function startNode() {
const node = await Libp2p.create({
modules: {
        transport: [WebSockets],
        connEncryption: [SECIO],
        streamMuxer: [MPLEX],
        peerDiscovery: [Bootstrap]
    },
config: {
        peerDiscovery: {
        autoDial: true,
        [Bootstrap.tag]: {
            enabled: true,
            list: bootstrapMultiaddrs
        }
    }
```

```
        }
    })
node.on('peer:discovery', (peer) => {
    console.log('Discovered %s', peer.id.toB58String())
})

node.on('peer:connect', (peer) => {
    console.log('Connected to %s', peer.id.toB58String())
})

 // start libp2p
    await node.start()
}

startNode()
```

Let's understand the code.

From line 1 to 5, we imported all the required modules with libp2p.

Then, we stored two peer addresses that are already running Libp2p (or IPFS), and we want to connect to those peers.

In the next line, we declared a function to contain all the working code and created a new libp2p instance:

```
const node = await Libp2p.create({
modules: {
transport: [WebSockets],
connEncryption: [SECIO],
streamMuxer: [MPLEX],
peerDiscovery: [Bootstrap]
    },
config: {
peerDiscovery: {
autoDial: true,
[Bootstrap.tag]: {
enabled: true,
list: bootstrapMultiaddrs
  }
```

```
        }
    }
})
```

As you can see, we included all the modules we need in the modules object, such as transport, encryption, peer discovery, and so on.

In the config object, we included the peers' addresses to connect with.

In the next two lines, we added two event listeners to listen for the events that are fired on pub/sub communication channels.

In the last line, we started our node.

Run the program using the following command to view the output of the code:

```
$ node app.js
```

It should display the following output:

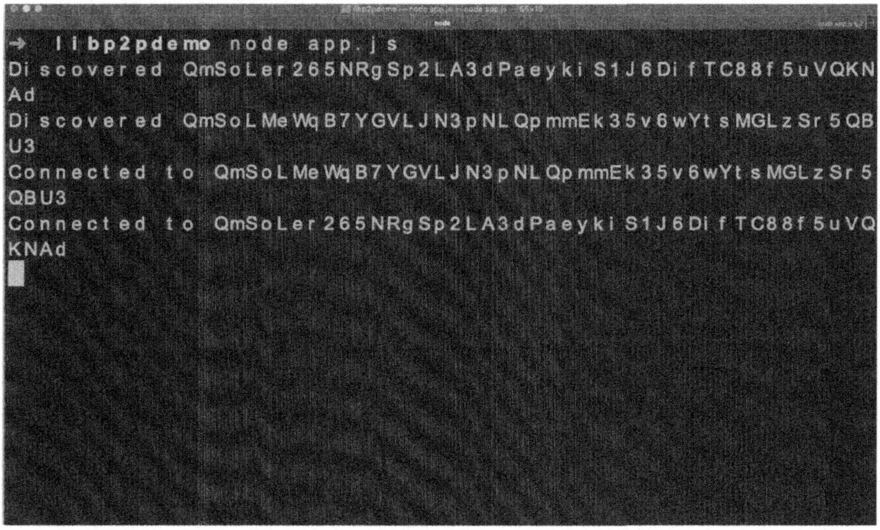

```
→  libp2pdemo node app.js
Discovered QmSoLer265NRgSp2LA3dPaeyki S1J6Di fTC88f 5uVQKNAd
Discovered QmSoLMeWqB7YGVLJN3pNLQpmmEk35v6wYt sMGLzSr 5QBU3
Connected to QmSoLMeWqB7YGVLJN3pNLQpmmEk35v6wYt sMGLzSr 5QBU3
Connected to QmSoLer265NRgSp2LA3dPaeyki S1J6Di fTC88f 5uVQKNAd
```

Figure 3.15

It means our peer is now connecting to other peers using Libp2p code. Amazing, isn't it?

Libp2p has other configuration parameters as well. You can check it out at the following link:

Link: **https://github.com/libp2p/js-libp2p/blob/master/doc/CONFIGURATION.md**

Libp2p is the core module of IPFS, and we just studied how to use it as an independent module.

Conclusion

In this chapter, we explored IPFS and its working. Then, we moved to IPFS installation and configuring it in our local system. We also studied the various concepts related to IPFS., and then we developed two important applications using IPFS to get a deeper understanding of IPFS and its usage. Finally, we moved to the libp2p framework to learn the core component of IPFS and its ecosystem.

In the upcoming chapters, we will learn about various decentralized database software.

References

- https://ipfs.io/
- https://docs.ipfs.io/
- https://www.cs.cmu.edu/~dga/15-744/S07/lectures/16-dht.pdf
- https://www.cs.umd.edu/~mwh/papers/gpads.pdf
- https://github.com/libp2p/js-libp2p

Decentralized Databases

CHAPTER 4
OrbitDB - Peer to Peer Distributed Database

OrbitDB is a peer-to-peer, serverless, distributed database built on top of IPFS. We have studied about IPFS in detail in the last chapter. In this chapter, we will learn about OrbitDB and how to use it to build decentralized applications.

Structure

We will cover the following topics in this chapter:
- Introduction to OrbitDB
- Installing OrbitDB
- OrbitDB data models
- Building DApps using OrbitDB

Objective

After studying this chapter, you will be able to:
- Use OrbitDB to build DApps.
- Learn about IPFS and OrbitDB.

- Build DApps using OrbitDB.

Let's get started!

Introduction to OrbitDB

Here's the definition according to the OrbitDB project page:

"OrbitDB is a serverless, distributed, peer-to-peer database. OrbitDB uses IPFS as its data storage and IPFS Pubsub to automatically sync databases with peers. It's an eventually consistent database that uses CRDTs for conflict-free database merges, making OrbitDB an excellent choice for decentralized apps (dApps), blockchain applications and offline-first web applications."

That's a very technical definition, isn't it? Well, let's break it down further to understand better:

- OrbitDB is serverless, which means you don't need to maintain a database server when using OrbitDB, unlike other database software. It's provided as a module for various programming languages.
- OrbitDB is distributed; it is designed as a peer-to-peer database with no centralized server.
- OrbitDB uses IPFS as a storage system. OrbitDB acts as a layer between the IPFS and programming interface.
- OrbitDB is a peer-to-peer database, and to synchronize the changes in the peer to other peers, it uses IPFS publish/subscribe system to communicate with other peers.
- OrbitDB uses the eventual consistency model; it's the consistency model in which the latest updated version of the data item is returned to the user, maintaining the availability and consistency of data. To achieve this eventual consistency, OrbitDB uses **Conflict-free Replicated Data Types (CRDTs)**.
- OrbitDB is packaged as a Node.js library. JavaScript was chosen because of its popularity and ubiquity in the programming community, and for its interoperability with the JavaScript implementation of IPFS, called `js-ipfs`.

Note: At the time of writing this book, OrbitDB is still in the development mode.

Let's move on to the installation of OrbitDB.

Installing OrbitDB

OrbitDB is a serverless application, so you do not need to run a server as we do for other databases like MySQL. However, we require IPFS in our system to use OrbitDB because IPFS is used as a file system to store records.

Let's install OrbitDB in our application.

Here's the command to install OrbitDB and IPFS in our project:

```
npm install orbit-dbipfs-api
```

You can perform this installation in your project.

Once installed, you can use the following code to connect to the IPFS and create an OrbitDB data store:

```
const IPFS = require('ipfs-api');
const OrbitDB = require('orbit-db');

const ipfsOptions = { host: 'localhost', port: '5001' };

async function main() {
    // Create IPFS instance
    const ipfs = new IPFS(ipfsOptions);
    console.log('Connected to IPFS');
    const orbitdb = await OrbitDB.createInstance(ipfs)
    console.log('OrbitDB instance created.')
}
main();
```

Upon execution of the preceding program, you should get the following output:

```
$ node app.js
$ Connected to IPFS
$ OrbitDB instance created.
```

Awesome!

Now, we can create a new database or load an existing database and use it to build our decentralized application.

Before we move towards building our application, we should learn the data models offered by OrbitDB.

OrbitDB Data Models

OrbitDB provides various types of databases for different types of data models; here are the following data models:

- Log
- Feed
- Key-value
- Docs
- Counter

Let's look at each data model in brief.

Log

It's an immutable data model used to store traversable records. One of the use cases for such types of data models is a message queue where messages are stored in the order and traversed back to the starting index, record by record.

The log is an immutable data store, so data cannot be altered once it is written.

To create a log store, refer to the following code:

```
constdb = await orbitdb.eventlog('users');
const hash = await db.add({ name: 'John' });

// to return all logs
const allRecords = db.iterator({ limit: -1 }).collect().map((e) =>e.payload.value);

console.log(allRecords); // prints all the logs

// return only specific record
const record = db.get(hash).map((e) =>e.payload.value);

console.log(record); // prints specific log
```

Let's look over the next data model—Feed.

Feed

This is a mutable version of the log data model. In the feed data model, you can store the record and traverse back to it just like we were doing in the log data model.

We can alter the records in the Feed data store. Let's look at an example:

```
constdb = await orbitdb.feed('users');

// add new record in the data model
const hash = await db.add({ name: 'John' });

const singleUserData = db.get(hash).map((e) =>e.payload.value);
console.log(singleUserData); // print single record

// remove records using the hash
const hash = await db.remove(hash)

const allRecords = db.iterator({ limit: -1 }).collect().map((e) =>e.payload.value);

console.log(allRecords); // prints all the record
```

The feed data model can be used for a variety of purposes, such as shopping carts, blogs, tweets, or any application that requires user-generated feed of data with a feature to traverse the records.

Let's look at the next data model—the key-value data model.

Key-value

The key-value store, as the name suggests, lets you store data in the key-value format. The usage of the key-value data store is vast and can be used in the range of applications.

Let's look at an example:

```
constdb = await orbitdb.keyvalue('users');

// add new key value data
const hash = await db.put('1', { name: 'Shahid' });

// You can also do the above operation using a set() function
const hash = await db.set('1', { name: 'Shahid' });

// fetch the information using the key
const value = db.get('1');
```

```
console.log(value);  // prints the data i.e {name: 'Shahid'}
// delete the data using the key
const hash = await db.del('1');
```

Let's look at the next and one of the most commonly used data models—Docs.

Docs

As the name suggests, it's a document-based data model where we can store custom documents and index it using custom fields. If you are familiar with MongoDB or ElasticSearch, this data model will be very useful for you.

You can use the Docs data mode to build custom database applications, blogs, eCommerce applications, and so on.

We will also use the Docs data model to build our decentralized application in the upcoming section.

Let's look at the example code:

```
const db = await orbitdb.docs('db.users');

// add new record
const hash = await db.put({ _id: 'hash of the record',
name: 'Shahid', followers: 500, following:120,
profilePicture: 'hash of the image probably IPFS' });

// fetch the record
const profile = db.get('hash of the record');

// delete the record
const hash = await db.del('hash of the record');

// fetch all the record
const allProfiles = db.get('');
```

By default, the index is on the _id field of the document; you can change it by specifying the index. Check out the following example:

constdb = await orbitdb.docs('db.users', {indexBy: 'name'});

You can run the custom query to fetch the documents, just like we do in other databases.

Check out the following example:

```
const all = db.query((doc) =>doc.followers>= 500);
// should returns all the users who have followers equal to or more than 500
```

The docs data model is quite useful and generic and can be shaped to support any application.

Let's learn about the last data model—Counter.

Counter

This data model, as the name suggests, is useful for datastore where numeric count records are required such as queues, and so on.

Let's consider an example to understand better:

```
const counter = await orbitdb.counter('db.user.counter');

// print counter value
console.log(counter.value);

//increment counter value
counter.inc();   // increment by 1
counter.inc(5);  // increment by 5
```

It's as simple as this. Create a data store and increment the value.

In my personal experience, I have not built any apps using this datastore, but I think it can be useful where queues are required, such as takeaway restaurants and railway ticket counters.

Till now, we have studied how OrbitDB works and the core concepts. It's time to build an application to learn the practicality of OrbitDB.

Building DApps using OrbitDB

Let's build our full-fledged decentralized application using OrbitDB and IPFS. We will build an email software that runs on a peer-to-peer network; let's call it DMail or Decentralized Mail.

Before we go into the application's technical aspects, let me show you how it looks.

Here's the home page of our application:

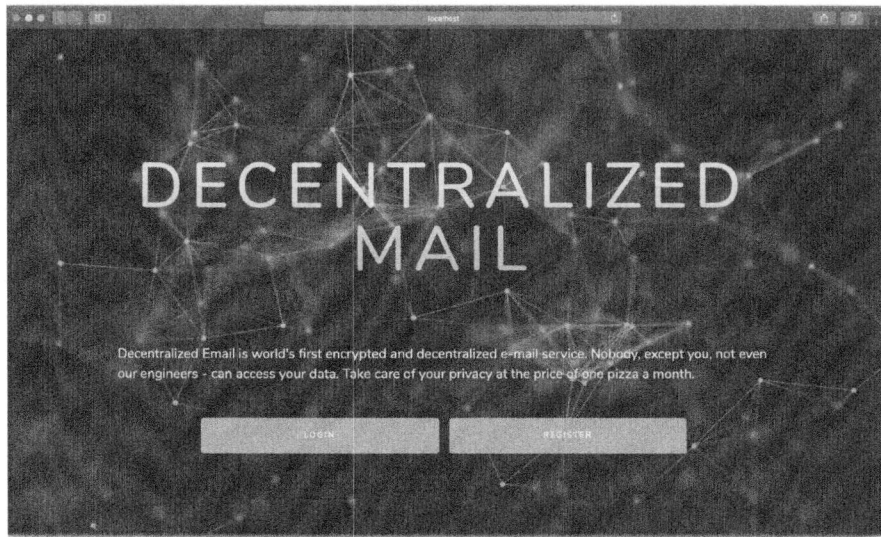

Figure 4.1

Here's the inbox page where users can read their emails:

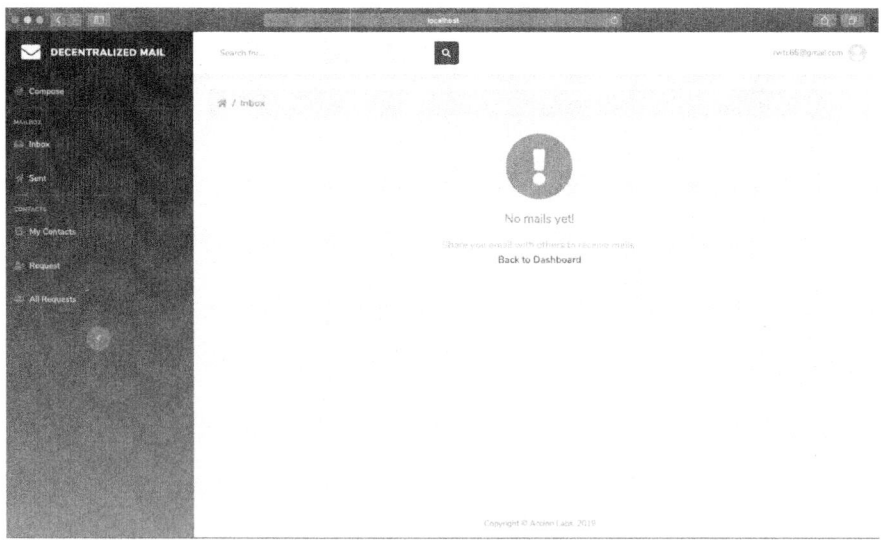

Figure 4.2

Users can compose a new email on the following screen, just like with *Gmail* or any other web-based email application:

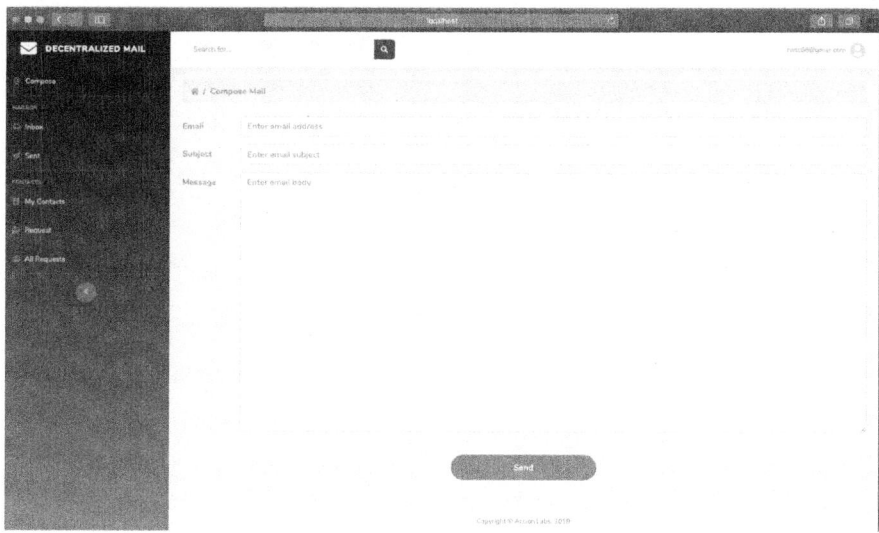

Figure 4.3

Here, users can check the contacts and add/delete new contacts:

Figure 4.4

I hope you're excited about the application. Let's first check the technologies we used.

Technologies

Here is our technology stack:
- **Front-end:** HTML, CSS, JavaScript, and jQuery library
- **Backend:** OrbitDB, IPFS
- **Middle layer:** Node.js

We are using Node.js to handle the API system so that the front-end can communicate with the database, and the OrbitDB document store data model to store users' information and email information.

Let's look over the architecture of the application.

Architecture

We are building a peer-to-peer email application. In this approach, we are sharing the same database across every peer. To do that, we first need to create a database in a genesis peer, and all other peers have to copy the same database.

Once genesis peer and database are created, another peer can copy the same database and changes will be synchronized using the IPFS publish-subscribe technique that we studied earlier.

Our email technology is also a little different from traditional email systems. In a traditional system, we use the **Simple Message Transfer Protocol (SMTP)** to send and receive emails.

In our system, we use the IPFS pub/sub to synchronize changes so that everyone has the same copy of the data, so the emails sent/received would be synchronized.

In a traditional system, you can send emails to anyone if you have their email address. In our system, you can only send emails to users added in your contacts, and whose public key you have.

We encrypt the email using the public key of the receiver and private key of the sender to make it ultra-secure. Only the receipt with the proper private key can decrypt the email and view the content.

It is a very important concept in a peer-to-peer system, where anyone can become a part of the network and view your data. One must ensure that it's secure and not easy to access.

The Node.js server handles our front-end, and the node itself handles the rest of the communication with the database.

Let's look at the project directory:

- `node_modules`: folder contains the required modules for the project.
- `orbitdb`: folder contains the database files.
- `views`: folder contains the front-end files.
- `utils`: folder contains the reusable code across the application.
- `dbaddress.js`: file contains the database address.
- `index.js`: contains the server code.
- `db.js`: contains the database-related code.
- `package.json`: contains all the packages required.

Let's understand the code that is coming up next. Since the codebase is large, everything is not pasted here. We will understand the important piece of code and how to run the program. For any doubts about code that is not explained in this chapter, readers can reach out to the writer.

First, let me explain how we are creating a database in a genesis peer and handling the pub/sub between multiple nodes.

Open the `db.js` file and check out the following code.

First, we are importing the required modules required to handle databases:

```
const IPFS = require('ipfs-api');
const OrbitDB = require('orbit-db');
const uuid = require('uuid/v4');
const bcrypt = require('bcrypt');
const fs = require('fs');
const Identities = require('orbit-db-identity-provider');
```

We are creating a function called loadDB(), where we add the required code to make the connection with the database and load it in the memory:

```
async function loadDB() {

..........
}
```

To enable pub/sub so that our nodes can talk to each other, we are passing the following parameters in the IPFS configuration:

```
EXPERIMENTAL: {
    pubsub: true
  },
relay: {
    enabled: true,
    hop: {
        enabled: true, active: true
    }
},
```

Then, we are checking whether this node is a genesis node, that is, the first node in the system. We are checking this by loading the dbaddress.js file. If this file exists, we are loading the databases written in the file:

```
fs.access(filePath, fs.F_OK, async (err) => {
if(err) {
        // file does not exist, create a new database and load it.
    }
        // file does exists, load the databases
});
```

If the file does not exist, we assume that it is a genesis node. We are then creating the new databases and writing the address of each database in the dbaddress.js file:

```
userDb = await orbitdb.create('email.user', 'docstore',{
accessController: {
          write: ['*']
     }
 });
userContactsDb = await orbitdb.create('email.user.
contacts','docstore', {
accessController: {
          write: ['*']
     }
 });
userEmailsDb = await orbitdb.create('email.user.data',
'docstore', {
        accessController: {
          write: ['*']
     }
 });
let fileContents = {
        "user": userDb.address.toString(),
         "contacts": userContactsDb.address.toString(),
         "emails": userEmailsDb.address.toString()
}
// write the db file
fs.writeFileSync(filePath, JSON.stringify(fileContents));
```

If the file exists, we are making the connection to the database using the open() function provided by OrbitDB. We pass the database address as a parameter to the function:

```
let fileData = fs.readFileSync(filePath,'utf-8');
let config = JSON.parse(fileData);
console.log('Databases exists, loading them in memory\n');
userDb = await orbitdb.open(config.user);
userContactsDb = await orbitdb.open(config.contacts);
userEmailsDb = await orbitdb.open(config.emails);
```

To load the database in the memory, we are using the `load()` function of OrbitDB:

```
userDb.load();
userContactsDb.load();
userEmailsDb.load();
```

Once the database is loaded, we are assigning an event to each database. When all databases are ready, we can proceed ahead. In our codebase, we are adding more event listeners to check the working of the database:

```
userDb.events.on('ready', () => {
    console.log('user database is ready.')
});

userContactsDb.events.on('ready', () => {
    console.log('user contacts database is ready.')
});

userEmailsDb.events.on('ready', () => {
    console.log('user emails database is ready.')
 });
```

In the end, we are calling our function when the server starts loading the database in the memory:

```
// load the database
loadDB();
```

Once the database is created, the `dbaddress.js` file or the address of the database can be shared with other nodes so that they can become a part of the network.

This is how we create and load the OrbitDB database for our decentralized email application.

There are other functions in the `db.js` file that deal with various aspects of the application, such as login, signup, creating an email, and reading an email. Let's see how we create an email and read an email using a public/private key combination.

But first, let's look at the code that generates the public and private key pairs. In the `utils` folder, check the code in `genkey.js`:

```
const crypto = require('asymmetric-crypto');

function generateKeys() {
    let pair = crypto.keyPair();
    return {
        privateKey: pair.secretKey,
        publicKey: pair.publicKey
    }
}

module.exports = generateKeys;
```

We are using the asymmetric-crypto node module to create a new pair of public and private keys on a random basis. We can also create a public and private key pair by using the input seeds.

We are using the same module to encrypt and decrypt the email. You can check the code placed in the **utils** folder:

```
const crypto = require('asymmetric-crypto');

function encryptEmail(data, pair) {
try {
    let encryptedEmail = crypto.encrypt(data, pair.publicKey, pair.privateKey);
    return encryptedEmail;
    }
catch(e) {
    console.log('error occurred in encrypting email');
    return null;
    }
}

module.exports = encryptEmail;
```

Here, we are using the public and private key pair passed to the function to encrypt the data, which is our email.

We are also performing the decryption of e-mails using the following code:

```
const crypto = require('asymmetric-crypto');

function decryptEmail(emailData, keys) {
try {
     let result = crypto.decrypt(emailData.email,
emailData.signature,      keys.senderPublicKey, keys.
privateKey);
     return result;
   }
catch(e) {
     console.log(e);
     return null;
   }
}

module.exports = decryptEmail;
```

In the decryption part, we are using the public key associated with the email and receiver private key to decrypt the email. This way, you can only read the email associated with your public key. This, in turns, makes the data very secure and less prone to interception.

Let's look over the server code. Open the index.js file and check out the code.

First, as usual, we are importing all the modules we require:

```
const express = require("express");
const bodyParser = require("body-parser");
const redis = require("redis");
const session = require("express-session");
const redisStore = require("connect-redis")(session);
const cookieParser = require("cookie-parser");
const app = express();
const client = redis.createClient();
const router = express.Router();
const db = require("./db");
```

To make our application secure, we are using sessions to maintain the user data in the browser securely.

To store the session information in the server, we are using Redis, which is a key-value store. The reason why we are using Redis and not using the session store in OrbitDB is because of the peer-to-peer nature.

We don't want to share the session of one user to other peers. If we do that, there is a chance that hackers can hijack the sessions and get crucial information out of it.

Redis runs on each node and maintains the sessions for the users connected to that node only. Here's the code where we are using Redis as a session store:

```
// session middleware
app.use(
    session({
        secret: "some-random-words",
        store: new redisStore({
        host: "localhost",
        port: 6379,
        client: client,
        ttl: 10000
    }),
    saveUninitialized: false,
    resave: false
    });
);
```

Redis runs on the **6379** port by default. If you have changed it, make the change in the code as well.

Once the user performs the log-in operation, we simply set the session for that request using the following code:

```
 // set session
req.session.key = {
userId: response.data.userId,
email: response.data.email,
publicKey: response.data.publicKey
 };
```

We are storing the information such as user id, email address, and public key to identify the user on each request.

To check whether the session is set for the request, we check whether the session key exists:

```
if (req.session.key) {
    // user is logged in
} else {
    // invalid user, redirect to login page
}
```

All the front-end code is placed in the view folder. The codebase is simple; we use plain and simple JavaScript to make the API calls and change the screen.

You can run the app using the following command:

```
$ node index.js
```

You should see the terminal screen similar to the following screenshot:

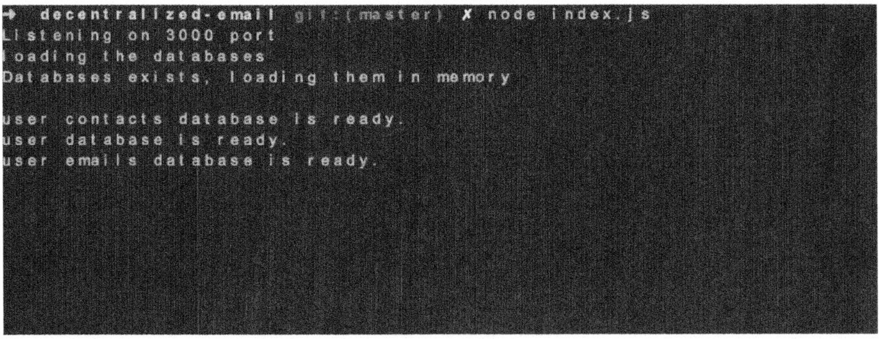

```
→ decentralized-email git:(master) ✗ node index.js
Listening on 3000 port
loading the databases
Databases exists, loading them in memory
user contacts database is ready.
user database is ready.
user emails database is ready.
```

Figure 4.5

If you are running it the first time, you will get different console messages because of genesis peer operation.

Navigate your browser to localhost:3000 if you are running it in the local machine or a server address if you are running it on the server.

It would help if your screen is similar to what we have shown above at the starting of this section. An interesting thing about our application is that you can only send and receive an email if you both participate in the contact sharing operation.

Create two users using the signup page and then send a contact request to one of the users:

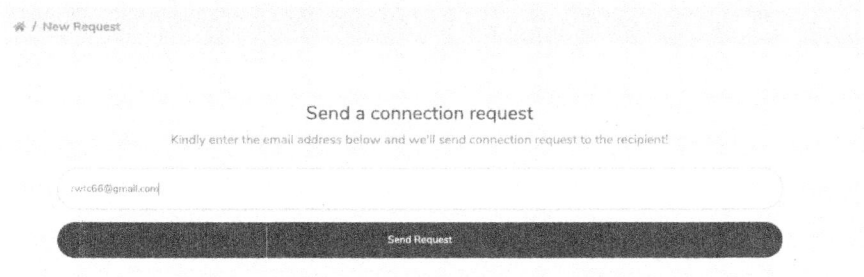

Figure 4.6

Once you send the request, log in to the second user account and accept the request:

Figure 4.7

Once you have accepted the request, the mutual agreement has been established. You can send and receive an email between these users.

You can view the user on your **Contacts** page:

Figure 4.8

120 ■ *Building Decentralized Blockchain Applications*

Let's send a test email between the users. Compose a new email and send it to the user. You can refer to the following screenshot and see how we are sending it to the user:

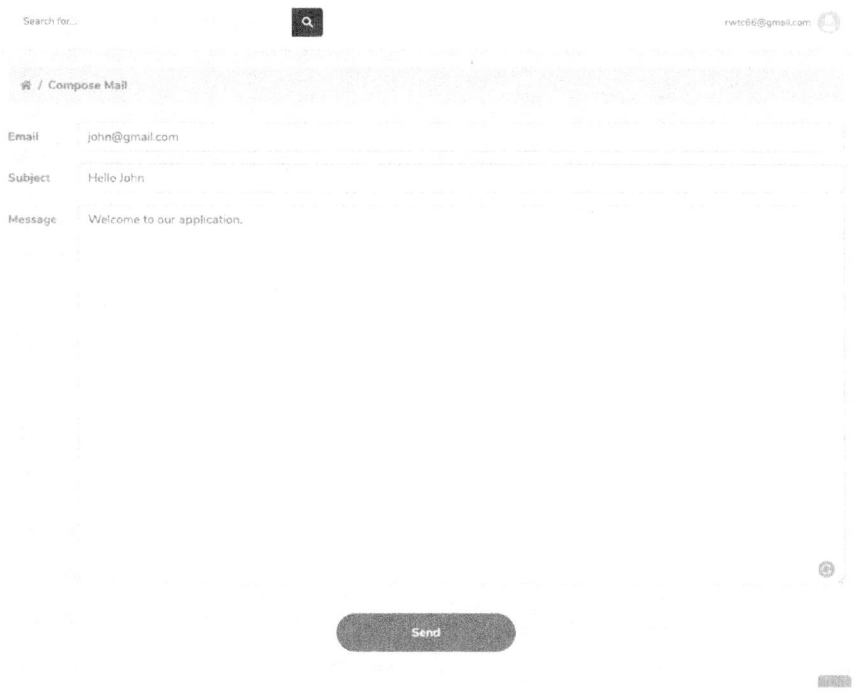

Figure 4.9

Once you have sent the email, log in to the other user account and view the email:

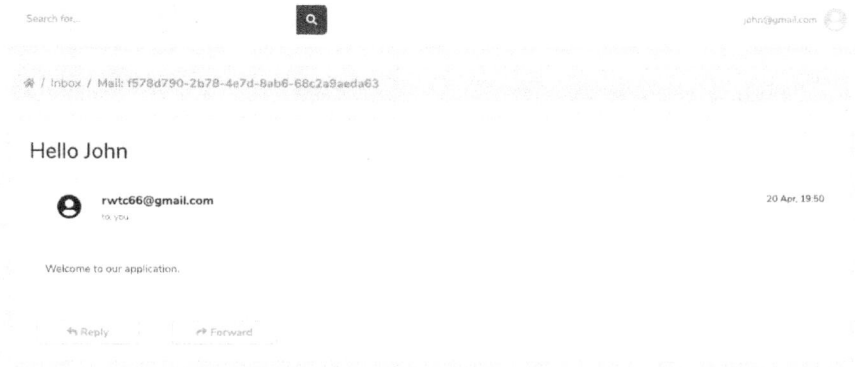

Figure 4.10

In the back end, we checked and decrypted the email using the private and public key combination, as we explained earlier.

I hope you got the gist of building a fully-fledged decentralized application using OrbitDB.

Conclusion

OrbitDB is one of the key projects in the decentralized application space. The development of this project is crucial for decentralized movement and to make developers transition to the new development stack with a little learning curve. We studied about OrbitDB and the various data models offered by it. We also learned about the OrbitDB installation and how to use it in your project. Moving forward, we build an end-to-end application using OrbitDB as a database and IPFS as a file system.

In the next chapter, we will learn about another popular database that runs on top of the blockchain—BigChainDB.

CHAPTER 5
BigchainDB

BigchainDB is the open-source database software that provides blockchain features such as decentralization, immutability, and peer-to-peer ownership, and database features such as high transaction rate, low latency, indexing, and querying.

Structure

We will cover the following topics in this chapter:
- Introduction to BigchainDB
- BigchainDB features
- BigchainDB use cases
- Running a BigchainDB node

Objective

After studying this chapter, you will be able to:
- Learn the basics of BigchainDB
- Learn how BigchainDB works

- Run a BigchainDB node

Let's get started!

Introduction to BigchainDB

BigchainDB is referred to as the blockchain database that provides the features of Blockchain and traditional database software.

BigchainDB provides blockchain features such as:

- **Decentralization:** No central authority and ownership.
- **Immutability:** Data cannot be altered once written in the BigchainDB.
- **Peer-to-peer network** - BigchainDB provides test and live networks.

BigchainDB provides database features such as:

- **Low latency** - Fast response time due to low latency network calls.
- **Indexing** - Data ingestion into the Blockchain.
- **Querying** - Finding data in the chain.
- **High transaction rate** - Fast in terms of indexing and querying.

You can see the BigchainDB characteristics in the following table:

	Typical blockchain	Typical distributed database	BigchainDB
Decentralization	✓		✓
Byzantine fault tolerance	✓		✓
Immutability	✓		✓
Ownership of assets	✓		✓
High transaction rate		✓	✓
Low latency		✓	✓
Indexing and querying of structured data		✓	✓

Table 5.1

As you can see, BigchainDB is a club of Blockchain and distributed databases to provide a solution that is a need of the hour.

Let's go through each of the features of BigchainDB.

Decentralization

BigchainDB is a decentralized database. BigchainDB uses Tendermint to achieve decentralization and reach consensus between various peers. Tendermint is a consensus software, using which we can develop and build secure decentralized software with byzantine fault-tolerance consensus.

To perform fast indexing and querying, each BigchainDB node runs and manages its own local MongoDB instance. MongoDB is a popular NoSQL database. The communication between nodes is achieved using Tendermint protocols.

BigchainDB is a decentralized database, which means there should be no central point of failure. To achieve that, BigchainDB node is a self-owned and self-operated entity. Since there is no single owner of the network, if one node fails, other nodes will maintain the network.

BigchainDB nodes can be and are located in many geographical places across the globe. The local legal jurisdiction and cloud providers work differently in every country, so an issue with one node or collective nodes in a country of concern (such as China or North Korea) doesn't affect them all.

Due to this decentralization, even if a node stops responding to requests and eventually fail, the rest of the network will continue to operate. In fact, up to one-third of the BigchainDB nodes can fail, and the rest of the network will still work.

Immutability

BigchainDB is an immutable database, which means information can't be altered or erased once added successfully in a BigchainDB network, at least not without investing great computing/hashing power, which is very difficult and time- and money-consuming. If some data somehow manages to get changed or erased, that is detectable in the network and results in a great level of data integrity and fault tolerance.

BigchainDB does not provide any API that allows us to change or modify the existing data. It is one of the approaches used by BigchainDB to maintain data immutability.

In BigchainDB, every node has a full copy of all the data in a locally managed MongoDB database instance. Hence, there is no single MongoDB database as a point of failure, just like we handle data in Bitcoin or other decentralized systems.

If one or more BigchainDB nodes are corrupted or destroyed due to various reasons, the other nodes won't be affected and will still have a copy of all the data that can be later used to rebuild the corrupted node.

To maintain the integrity of the data up to the standard, all the transactions in BigchainDB are cryptographically signed. After a transaction is stored, changing its data will change the signature, which can be easily detected due to signature mismatch.

Owner-controlled Assets

BigchainDB stores and exchanges information in the form of assets. Assets could be anything ranging from currency to house to simple chairs.

BigchainDB has in-built support for owner-controlled assets, that is, only the owner (or owners) of an asset can transfer it to other entities. The owners are typically users with a set of private keys. Owner-controlled assets cannot be transferred by anyone else, not even by the node operator.

There's only one built-in asset in blockchains like Bitcoin or Ethereum, but BigchainDB lets users create as many exclusive assets as they need. Users can't create assets that appear to be already present in the network, maintaining the ownership of assets and the integrity of the existing data.

BigchainDB always validates every transaction to ensure that it's not trying to transfer a value that was already transferred by another transaction; that is, it prevents double-spending.

High Transaction Rate

BigchainDB provides a high transaction rate. As mentioned earlier, BigchainDB runs on the tendermint, so the performance stats are very much the same.

Tendermint processes thousands of transactions per second in a distributed network, which is impressive.

Low Latency and Fast Finality

BigchainDB provides low latency; that is, it adds new blocks in the network instantly. BigchainDB claims that they usually take only a few seconds (or less) for a transaction to be included in a new block, which is impressive.

Once a block is added in the BigchainDB network, it is replicated across the peers; once done, there's no way it can be changed or revoked.

Indexing and Querying Structured Data

As I have mentioned earlier, each node in a BigchainDB network has its own local MongoDB database instance. Each node has access to the full power of MongoDB for indexing and querying the stored data (transactions, assets, metadata, and blocks, all of which are JSON objects).

The data ownership goes to the node owner, and they are free to decide how much of that data they want to expose to external users. For example, one node owner might decide to index geospatial and geographical data and offer optimized geospatial queries via a REST API. In contrast, another operator might decide to offer a GraphQLAPI. It's totally up to the node owners.

MongoDB, being a NoSQL database, is very powerful in terms of storing information and querying it.

Let's explore the use cases of BigchainDB.

BigchainDB Use Cases

BigchainDB is immutable, decentralized database software that can serve a large number of use cases. BigchainDB can be used wherever there is a need for decentralized, immutable information representing any digital assets.

There are many industry sectors and organizations that can directly benefit from BigchainDB features. In this section, we will cover a few BigchainDB use cases.

Supply Chain

In a typical supply chain network, multiple parties are collaborating and exchanging information, goods, and assets.

The supply chain is a huge network of buyers and sellers, and they generate tons of data in the form of invoices, payment records, goods information, and so on. One of the major challenges faced by the supply chain network is the security of information passing through and between various entities involved in the supply chain.

As I mentioned earlier about the data generation capability of the supply chain, when the size of the chain grows, data grows exponentially. And with data growth, the complexity of the systems grows as well.

To handle the size of the data supply chain generated while maintaining transparency and security of assets, we need a system like Blockchain with immutable data stores that cannot be modified by anyone except the owner of the asset.

One of the core concerns with the decentralized database or blockchain technologies is latency. Due to the widespread use of the network, databases running on decentralized systems may take time to respond. That's where BigchainDB shines, bringing along its query capabilities and high throughput performance.

BigchainDB can be used in a supply chain use case to tackle the various issues we discussed earlier, mainly, data management and security. BigchainDB can handle large amounts of data while letting users run quick runtime queries.

Intellectual Property Rights Management

Blockchain proves to be the key solution for intellectual property rights management. For example, consider an artist creating art - be it musical, or painting, or anything else.

Blockchain technology, in general, has several features that can be used to provide proof to artists' claims over their assets. Once an art asset is registered on a blockchain with proper attribution, it can be used to prove the ownership of the IP rights.

One of the common events that occur in the IP is the sale and transfer of the assets from one owner to another based on various agreements. BigchainDB can be used to record assets and also transfer them between users.

Identity

Identity management is one of the most critical use cases when it comes to managing user-specific data, such as credentials, roles, access management, and so on.

Identity theft is a major concern today; we must ensure that the identity of a human or a machine is secure and temper-proof.

Identity management systems generate tons of data. Due to this large-scale data generation, we need a database that can scale according to the volume of the data.

BigchainDB has characteristics like decentralization, local MongoDB node for fast query and indexing, and immutability that makes BigchainDB a natural fit for identity management systems.

Internet of Things

Internet of things (IoT) is the digital representation of physical objects tha communicate with the network and inject data in the network in a periodic manner. IoT devices can be anything, and their data ingestion can generate petabytes of data. To handle this amount of information, we need a high-throughput, fast, tamper-resistant system that can also provide quick results. That's where BigchainDB comes in.

Data Governance

Data governance is always a controversial issue. In a democratic country like India, USA, and UK, the data generated by people is always the concern for governments and other agencies due to various reasons. To bring data governance into effect without making people feel that they are being monitored, there is no other solution than the Blockchain.

BigchainDB can be used to handle such a large amount of data while allowing the government to watch over assets transfer and take action when necessary.

Audit Trails

Audit trails are the records of every action being performed in the system or network of systems. BigchainDB can be used on Audit trails as they are a natural fit.

Audit trails are used in banking, supply chain, utility market, access control, and so on. Due to a large amount of data generation and the nature of the record, BigchainDB can be used to store, manage, query audit trails records.

Let's proceed and set up the BigchainDB node in your local system.

Running a BigchainDB Node

BigchainDB requires a MongoDB instance running in your system. So before installing and running BigchainDB, we need to install and configure MongoDB in our system.

Visit the official website of MongoDB and download the software according to the operating system you have.

Once MongoDB is installed, run the MongoDB daemon process using the following command:

```
mongod --dbpath=.
```

You can change the path of the MongoDB dbpath variable if you want to store the data at different locations.

Once MongoDB is running, we can install the BigchainDB in our system using the following command:

```
sudo pip3 install bigchaindb
```

If there is an error related to installation, you should update your Python software to troubleshoot.

After installation, you can run the following command to start the BigchainDB server:

bigchaindb -y configure mongodb

Start the BigchainDB server:

bigchaindb start

Now, navigate to http://localhost:9984 to verify the BigchainDB installation.

You should get the following response:

```
{
  "api": {
    "v1": {
      "assets": "/api/v1/assets/",
      "docs": "https://docs.bigchaindb.com/projects/server/en/v1.2.0/http-client-server-api.html",
      "outputs": "/api/v1/outputs/",
      "statuses": "/api/v1/statuses/",
      "streams": "ws://localhost:9985/api/v1/streams/valid_transactions",
      "transactions": "/api/v1/transactions/"
    }
  },
  "docs": "https://docs.bigchaindb.com/projects/server/en/v1.2.0/",
  "keyring": [
    "6qHyZew94NMmUTYyHnkZsB8cxJYuRNEiEpXHe1ih9QX3",
    "AdDuyrTyjrDt935YnFu4VBCVDhHtY2Y6rcy7x2TFeiRi"
  ],
  "public_key": "NC8c8rYcAhyKVpx1PCV65CBmyq4YUbLysy3Rqrg8L8mz",
  "software": "BigchainDB",
  "version": "1.2.0"
}
```

Congratulations! BigChainDB is successfully installed in your system.

Conclusion

BigchainDB is a powerful and promising software that can bring the best of both the worlds—Blockchain and traditional databases—which is the need of the hour. We studied the features of BigchainDB and its various use cases. We also studied how to set up a simple BigchainDB node for local development.

In the next chapter, we will study another blockchain-based database called **tiesDB**.

CHAPTER 6
TiesDB

TiesDB is open-source database software that provides blockchain features such as decentralization and peer-to-peer networking, and database features such as high transaction rate, low latency, indexing, and querying. TiesDB is a mutable database, so we can alter the data stored in the database.

Structure

We will cover the following topics in this chapter:
- Introduction to TiesDB
- TiesDB features
- TiesDB use cases
- Running a TiesDB node

Objective

After studying this chapter, you will be able to:
- Learn the basics of TiesDB
- Learn how TiesDB works

- Run a TiesDB node

Let's get started.

Introduction to TiesDB

TiesDB is a decentralized database software. It has neither a single point of failure nor a single point of control. All TiesDB nodes are equal in terms of control and power.

So, in practice, TiesDB is a cloud-based database network running on computing machines provided by community members. The network participants range from enthusiasts to standard companies; so, TiesDB nodes do not belong to a single organization. This is why there is no single point of control and failure.

TiesDB network consists of the following entities:
- **Node:** A node is a participant of the network that stores and transmits data provided by users for an incentive. The node receives an incentive from the user for the work being done.
- **Coordinator:** A coordinator is a participant of the database network that accepts incoming requests, validates the format of input data, transfers it to the nodes, and combines the results to send the response to the user.

  It can be represented by a node or client software. The coordinator receives an incentive for the performed work from the nodes. If the user's client acts as a coordinator, the incentive will be returned to the user after the nodes pay off their dues.
- **User:** A user provides data to be stored in the decentralized database and requests data for processing. The user pays incentives to the nodes for the work being done.
- **Client:** A client is a software tool that acts on behalf of the user, formats the provided data for storage and processing, and performs incentive settlements with the nodes.

Let's check out the exclusive features of TiesDB.

Features of TiesDB

TiesDB provides the following exclusive features:
- Verified identification

- Special data organization
- Incentive schemes
- Security

Verified Identification

Each user in the TiesDB network is provided with a unique ID that is associated with their private key. This unique ID is used throughout the transaction operation. Users use this key to sign their transactions and validate them. Without this key, users will not be able to change the document.

Special Data Organization

TiesDB organizes data in a public readable format. Every record in the network is associated with the user. Each record is replicated across the network and can be only modified by the owner of the record with the unique ID associated with the private key.

Incentive Schemes

TiesDB introduces incentive schemes using its coin named TIE token. Whenever a user wants to perform a query on the database, they have to pay for it in the form of TIE tokens. These tokens are paid to the nodes for their computational effort.

Security

TiesDB has a built-in security module. Permissions of the users are stored in the blockchain and distributed across a multitude of nodes across the globe. Each node owner makes security deposits before joining the network. Payment to nodes is also stored in the blockchain to avoid incentive conflict, but if it arises, it is also settled and recorded in the blockchain.

Let's check out the use cases of TiesDB.

TiesDB Use Cases

TiesDB can be used in the following scenarios:

- Distributed datastore
- File sharing
- Mass media
- Intellectual property rights
- Social networks
- Big data

Distributed Datastore

TiesDB, being a decentralized database software, can be used to build a global, permission restricted distributed data store. Companies can use TiesDB in the cloud servers to form a global network, allowing users to read information from their nearest servers via CDN, and allowing data owners to modify/update the information.

With the incentive in place, people don't have to worry about managing a network without any pay. Node owners will be paid based on the operations in the data.

File Sharing

Sharing a file securely without tampering it is a greater challenge these days. With censorship and government monitoring every move to every record on the Web, TiesDB can play a major role. A publicly owned, decentralized network of database nodes can be used to build a file-sharing system that is secure and mutable so that information can be updated by the owner and owned by the people.

Mass Media

News websites serving billions of people is an important and critical part of any democracy. With the proper system in place, there will be transparency in the news as well as the ownership of the news. TiesDB can be used to build a strong network of data stores of news to prevent theft and fake news.

Intellectual Property Rights

TiesDB has the potential to be the key solution for intellectual property rights management. For example, consider an artist creating art, be it musical, painting, or anything else.

TiesDB provides in-built security and ownership of the record; each record is signed and owned by the person. With such permissions and control, TiesDB can be used to store IP products.

Social Networks

The content created by the public runs social networks, but its content is owned by organizations.

TiesDB can be used to build a social network that is owned and managed by the people. With proper data ownership and security, there is little to zero chance of censorship and data control.

Big Data

TiesDB provides a database network that can be used to store tons of information and access it from anywhere. Big data solutions can be built on top of TiesDB networks.

TiesDB can provide a stream of information on big data analytics and other use cases.

Let's run the node of TiesDB.

Running a TiesDB Node

TiesDB uses an Ethereum network to maintain the internal data structures, and it requires an Ethereum client called *"geth"* (we installed it in *Chapter 2*) to run properly.

You can refer to *chapter 2* to install `geth`. Here, I am mentioning the steps required to install `geth` in my Mac operating system.

To install the Ethereum client or *geth*, run the following command:

`brew tap ethereum/ethereum`

`brew install ethereum`

Once installed, you can run the Ethereum testnet program in your machine using the following command:

`geth --rinkeby --datadir .rinkeby --cache 512 --rpc --rpcaddr 127.0.0.1 --syncmode "light"`

138 ■ *Building Decentralized Blockchain Applications*

Wait for a few minutes to let Ethereum sync the entire `testnet` chain.

Once it is synced, you can download and install the TiesDB program.

Note: At the time of writing this book, TiesDB is in the Alpha development release and not recommended for production systems.

Visit the TiesDB release page and download the latest version of TiesDB. TiesDB release page link: **https://github.com/TiesNetwork/ties.db/releases**

Once installed, extract the ZIP folder and switch to it using the terminal or command prompt.

Switch to the bin directory and run the following command:

`./tiesdb`

This command will initialize the TiesDB and open up the TiesDB application. It should look like this:

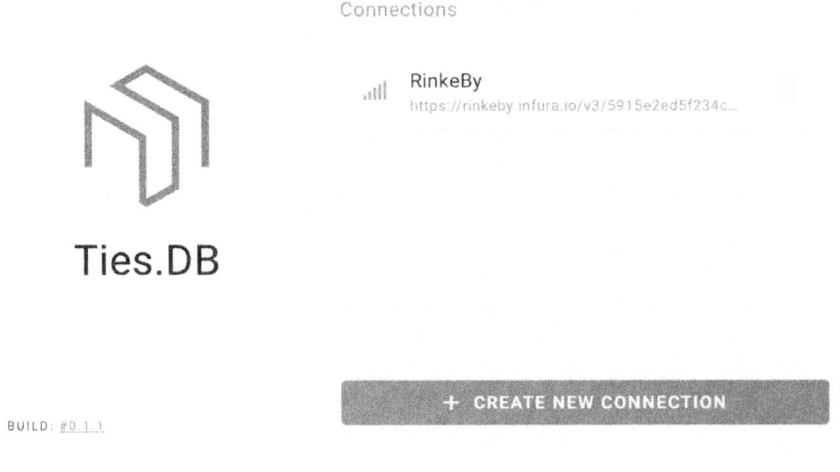

Figure 6.1

Choose the connection, and you should enter the database view. TiesDB is developing an excellent graphic user interface to help node owners manage the database easily.

It should look similar to the following screenshot:

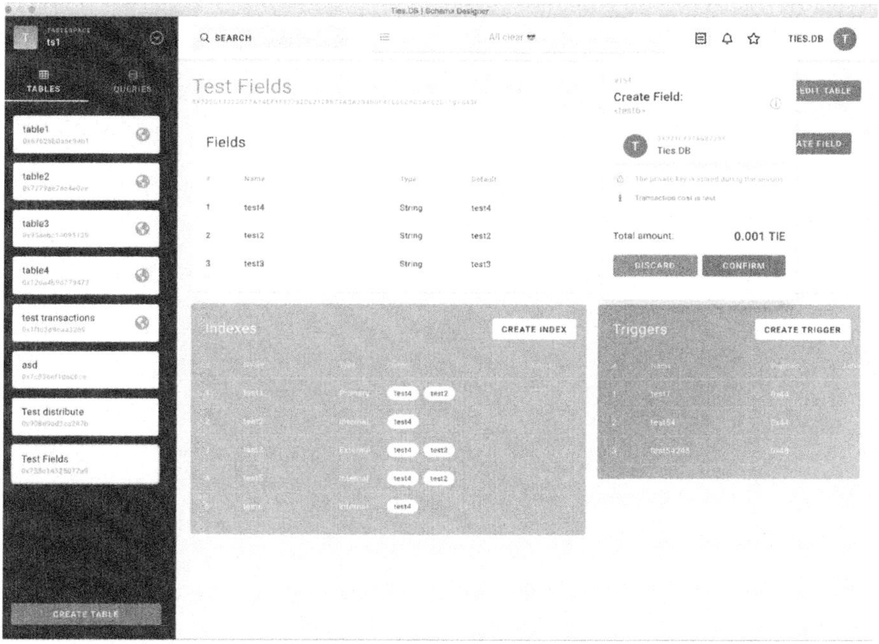

Figure 6.2

You can create multiple tables based on your need and let TiesDB do its magic to perform the synchronization across other nodes.

Conclusion

TiesDB looks promising in terms of the database for decentralized applications. With the solid security feature and ownership spreading across the Blockchain, TiesDB is a wise option for a wide array of applications in a multitude of domains.

In the next chapter, we will learn about another decentralized database called *Bluzelle*.

CHAPTER 7
Bluzelle

According to the official website introduction,

Bluzelle is a decentralized data network for dapps to manage data in a secure, tamper-proof, and highly scalable manner. Bluzelle is powered by Cosmos and its BFT technology Tendermint. Bluzelle is designed to be used by any dapp on any blockchain.

Bluzelle is not a database software; it's a decentralized network of database nodes scattered across the globe to provide secure database solutions for decentralized applications and DApps developers.

Structure

We will cover the following topics in this chapter:
- Introduction to Bluzelle
- Bluzelle features
- Bluzelle technology
- Bluzelle use cases
- Setting up a Bluzelle node

Objective

After studying this chapter, you will be able to:
- Learn the basics of Bluzelle
- Learn how Bluzelle works
- Learn how to set up a Bluzelle node

Let's get started.

Introduction to Bluzelle

Decentralized applications are on the rise. Due to this surge in the data (generated by both users and systems), there has to be an affordable and easy-to-use solution. As of now, developers can either use Ethereum to host the data solution, which is costly and slow, or they can use database solutions like OrbitDB to self-host the database.

To solve this problem, Bluzelle introduced the network of databases to provide secure, affordable database solutions to decentralized applications developers. The network is, in turn, controlled by public entities and not the corporation. The data generated is replicated across multiple nodes for free; so, even if one node is down, the data availability constraint is met.

Bluezelle network consists of the following entities:
- **Consumer:** Consumers are developers who *"consume"* the data present in the database network. Consumer pays Bluzelle tokens to store and read the data in the network.
- **Producer:** Producers provide their infrastructure to become a part of the Bluzelle network in the exchange of Bluzelle tokens. Producers have to provide a security deposit to become a part of the network.

Let's learn about the features of the Bluzelle database network.

Features of Bluzelle

Bluzelle provides the following features:
- Decentralized
- Mutable
- Global coverage

- Affordable
- Shared revenue model

Let's go through the features one by one.

Decentralized

Bluzelle is a decentralized database network; there is no single entity of control, so no single point of failure.

Bluzelle database network provides the blockchain level security of data and ownership. Bluzelle network is also publicly available and operated, so there is no centralized authority.

Mutable

As mentioned earlier, Bluzelle provides blockchain level security but does not store data as we do in the traditional blockchain. Bluzelle database network allows the owner of the data to perform the modification, so it's mutable.

Bluzelle stores and provides the data in the traditional database format. It drastically reduces the learning curve for developers jumping into decentralized application development from traditional development experience.

Global Coverage

At the time of writing this book, the Bluzelle network spans across North America, Europe, and Asia. It will soon expand throughout the world, providing real global coverage and replication of data. The security and validity of such decentralized networks depend on the strong peers scattered across the world.

Affordable

Due to the cost of Ethereum gas, it is costly to store information in the Ethereum blockchain. It was one of the primary reasons why Bluzelle came to reality. Bluzelle introduced its token named BLZ, which allows producers and consumers to earn/pay for the service. Consumers only pay for what they store/consume.

Shared Revenue Model

Bluzelle earns money from the consumers and distributes it to the producers who maintain the network. This shared revenue model attracts people to become part of the network and share the infrastructure in the exchange of Bluzelle tokens.

Let's look at the technical concepts of Bluzelle.

Bluzelle Technology

In Bluzelle, data is stored and replicated on a network of 13 or more nodes.

Each of these networks is called a database zone, and all zones are synced together. If one node is offline, the data is still available from another node.

The data is modified only with a consensus and only if ⅔ of the nodes agree. It ensures that the data is tamper-proof and cannot be altered without the consent of the network. The network can grow with demand, and more nodes can be added in the network when there is a need for more storage.

Bluzelle uses the following components to make the system work:
- Database engine
- Consensus engine
- Nodes
- Zone
- Bluzelle tokens
- Client library and proxy

Let's go through them one by one.

Database Engine

Bluzelle uses Cosmos software development kit to build a NoSQL key-value store database. Cosmos network is an open-source project that allows us to build decentralized networks on the Cosmos network.

Checkout Cosmos project - **https://github.com/cosmos/cosmos-sdk**

Consensus Engine

Bluzelel used *Tendermint* - a BFT based consensus engine to ensure that all the nodes remain in sync with each other and data availability is maintained across the network.

Check out the Tendermint project at **https://docs.tendermint.com/master/introduction/what-is-tendermint.html**.

Nodes

The core component of the Bluzelle network is a node. The network is operated by nodes provided by the public community. They provide the infrastructure and execute changes through consensus in return for a fee - Bluzelle tokens.

Zone

Bluzelle network nodes are grouped as a collection of nodes. There are three types of zones:

1. **Database zones:** The building blocks to provide capacity for the database network. More database zones are added as more capacity is required.
2. **Peg zone:** A special blockchain of nodes that provides a decentralized means to bridge the database zones with other networks like Ethereum.
3. **Hub zone:** Allows the database zones and peg zone to communicate with one another.

Bluzelle Tokens

The following are the two types of Bluzelle tokens:
- **BLZ:** Bluzelle tokens
- **BNT:** Bluzelle native tokens

BLZ is an ethereum based ERC-20 token that is easily obtained outside the Bluzelle network. It is used to gain entry into Bluzelle, where it is converted into the **Bluzelle Native Token (BNT)**.

Bluzelle native tokens are used to perform the payment inside the Bluzelle network.

Client Library and Proxy

Client library allows us to communicate with the network, and we can use a proxy to set the trust between the client and the network running behind the proxy.

Let's check out the use cases of the Bluzelle database network.

Bluzelle Use Cases

Bluzelle can be used for avariety of use cases. Here are a few use cases where we can use the Bluzelle database network:

- Prediction markets
- Currency exchange markets
- Data streaming networks

Prediction Markets

Prediction markets require lots of data to make predictions and decisions. For such a large amount of data and the ever-growing need of infrastructure, Bluzelle can provide a solid and powerful alternative to Ethereum to store data.

Currency exchange markets

Currency exchange required time-bound, fault tolerance database solution. By using a Bluzelle database, decentralized exchanges can be built that provide a strong and consistent database.

Data Streaming Networks

Real-time data streaming requires a huge infrastructure to maintain connections and transfer gigabytes of data from across the world. Such a real-time database requires strong infrastructure. Using public computing infrastructure such as Bluzelle with a strong consistency can be very useful in such applications.

Let's install the Bluzelle node in our system.

Setting Up a Bluzelle Node

Follow these steps to install Bluzelle node:

Note: You need to run these commands in the Ubuntu operating system.

1. Update the system.

    Run the following command to update the Ubuntu system:
    ```
    sudo apt-get update
    ```

    Now, install the dependencies required to run Bluzelle:
    ```
    sudo apt-get install build-essential jq
    ```

    Let's move to the next step.

2. Install Go and compile the project

    Install Go using the following command:
    ```
    wget https://dl.google.com/go/go1.14.linux-amd64.tar.gz
    sudo tar -C /usr/local -xzf go1.14.linux-amd64.tar.gz
    ```

Create the required directory:
```
mkdir -p ~/go/src/github.com/bluzelle
mkdir ~/go/bin
mkdir ~/go/pkg
cd ~/go/src/github.com/bluzelle
```

Clone the project:
```
git clone https://github.com/bluzelle/curium.git
```

Now, build the project using the following command:
```
make testnet
```

Once the project is compiled, you can run this command to verify the installation:
```
blzcli version --long
```

This command should generate the following output:
```
name: BluzelleService
server_name: blzd
client_name: blzcli
version: 0.0.0-24-g3253c8b
```

```
commit: 3253c8b6b4e40b125c0ccdfd6a81a06a02a5e018
build_tags: ledger,cosmos-sdk v0.37.4
go: go version go1.13.4 darwin/amd64
```

Now, to run the Bluzelle node, use the following command:
```
blzd init [moniker] [flags]
```

Consider this example:
```
blzd init curium00 --chain-id bluzelle 2>&1 | jq .node_id
```

Now, run the server.
```
blzd start
```

Great! Now we have the Bluzelle testnet node running in our system.

Conclusion

Bluzelle is promising database network software for decentralized applications development. Using Bluzelle, we can develop a variety of applications.

In the next chapter, we will learn about the last database of this book —*Amazon Quantum* ledger database.

CHAPTER 8
Amazon QLDB

Amazon quantum ledger database or **Amazon QLDB** is a fully managed (by Amazon) ledger database. Amazon QLDB offers central trusted authority ownership to the information present in the ledger. Amazon QLDB provides a transparent, immutable, and cryptographically verifiable transaction log of all your application changes.

Structure

In this chapter, we will cover the following topics:
- What is Amazon QLDB?
- Features of Amazon QLDB
- Use cases of Amazon QLDB
- How to use Amazon QLDB
- Amazon QLDB drivers

Objective

After studying this chapter, you will be able to:

- Learn the basics of Amazon QLDB
- Learn how to use Amazon QLDB in the AWS console
- Use drivers to connect to Amazon QLDB

Let's get started with the introduction.

What is Amazon QLDB?

As I stated earlier, Amazon QLDB is a fully managed ledger database. As a developer, you don't have to worry about the installation, configuration, and administration of the database. Amazon handles everything for you.

Unlike other decentralized databases we covered in the earlier chapters, Amazon QLDB is **centrally owned**, which means a single or group of authorities has ownership; hence, it is categorized as a private database.

Amazon QLDB provides an immutable ledger database; so data cannot be modified once it's written. If there is a need for modification, a new record is created, and history is maintained with the old and new record so that one can verify the changes.

Amazon QLDB is cryptographically secure. We can easily verify the records with the SHA256 hash and signature. We will learn how to do this in the current chapter.

Amazon QLDB is available in the Amazon web service console as a cloud service. Hence, you pay for what you use.

Amazon uses the SQL like query language to perform operations on the data. It is a welcome move for a large set of developers who want to use the immutable database with the blockchain functionality, but it gets passed on due to the learning curve.

Amazon QLDB also provides drivers for programming languages such as Java, .NET, JavaScript, and Python.

In the next section, we'll learn more about the features of Amazon QLDB.

Features of Amazon QLDB

Amazon QLDB provides the following set of features:
- Ledger database
- Immutable
- Cryptographically secure and verifiable
- SQL compatible query language
- High availability

Enterprise gradeLet's look at each feature closely.

Ledger Database

A transaction in a traditional database is generally stored in the database and tables. The database maintains the state of the transaction and takes actions in case of error or rollback situation.

The transaction log is a core component of the SQL database systems and plays an important role in replaying transactions in the event of system failure, disaster recovery, or data replication.

In traditional database systems, transaction logs are not **immutable** and serve a purpose in terms of transaction failure or rollback.

In Amazon QLDB, the ledger—structurally similar to a transaction log—is the core component of the database. The ledger is an immutable, append-only data structure that stores the transaction data, along with the associated metadata.

The ledger manages data like a SQL database; you can create a table and store your information inside the table.

Let's understand the next feature - immutable.

Immutable

Amazon QLDB is an immutable database that stores the records of all changes to the data that cannot be altered or modified in any case.

Once the data is committed and the history of the change is recorded in the system, there are no APIs or administration-level features available that can change the historical records.

Let's look at the next feature - cryptographically secure.

Cryptographically Secure

Amazon QLDB stores data in the blocks that are chained together with a cryptographically hashing function similar to blockchains. This hashing function ensures transactional data integrity using a cryptographic verification method.

For each transactional record, the QLDB provides a digest - a hash value that points to the full hash chain as of a point in time, along with the Merkle audit-proof.

Let's check out the next feature - SQL compatible query language.

SQL Compatible Query Language

Amazon QLDB provides SQL compatible query language. It shrinks the learning curve of the developers. Any database programmer familiar with the SQL can use Amazon QLDB in a short period. Amazon QLDB achieves this using **PartiQL** as its query language and **Amazon Ion** as its document-oriented data model.

PartiQL is an open-source, SQL-compatible query language. You can use PartiQL to insert, query, and manage your data with traditional SQL operators.

You can refer to it at **PartiQL Project homepage**.

Amazon Ion is similar to JSON, with more Amazon centric features.

Let's check the next feature - high availability.

High Availability

Amazon QLDB is a serverless run on the cloud and provides high availability using the battle-tested Amazon infrastructure.

Amazon automatically replicates the data across various AWS regions to support the availability and integrity of the data.

Enterprise-grade

Amazon QLDB meets the ACID (Atomicity, Consistency, Isolation, and Durability) properties. With this, Amazon QLDB is enterprise-grade and can be used with the production systems with almost zero faults.

Let's look at the use cases of Amazon QLDB.

Amazon QLDB Use Cases

Amazon QLDB can play a vital role in the following domains:
- Finance
- Manufacturing
- Insurance
- Payroll systems

Supply chainLet's explore, in brief, how QLDB can be used in the respected domains.

Finance

Banks and financial institutions run on a ledger to keep track of credit and debit transactions. Instead of building a complex ledger from scratch, we can use Amazon QLDB and focus on the business part instead of handling the technical aspects of the ledger.

Manufacturing

Manufacturing companies work on a supply chain system. Numerous parties are involved in the chain to produce and manufacture a simple item. A ledger database can play a key role in such a system to record transactions and historical records to avoid conflict and keep track of money, goods, and so on in the system.

Insurance

Insurance companies can use QLDB ledger to perform transparent claim resolution and store the history of the transaction. Ledger databases can be used to store the audit records as well and play a major role in conflict resolution between insurance companies and individuals.

Payroll Systems

Payroll systems record the history of transactions such, as salaries paid, insurance claim, and performance history. These records can be systematically maintained using QLDB and a ledger, and companies can stay transparent with the ownership of the records with the employees and other stakeholders.

Supply Chain

Supply chain management is among the most tedious tasks ever. There has to be a revolution in technology to support the wide audience playing a key role in the chain.

With the QLDB ledger, all the supply chain records can be stored as a history of the data with the proper changes records made by various parties. Parties in the supply chain often access data like the location of the item, the shipping details, who handles the shipment, and such. Amazon QLDB can play a major role in this field.

Let's learn how to use Amazon QLDB.

How to Use Amazon QLDB

To use Amazon QLDB, you need to have the amazon web service account. Create a new account on AWS if you do not have it already.

1. Click **here** to create a new account in AWS:

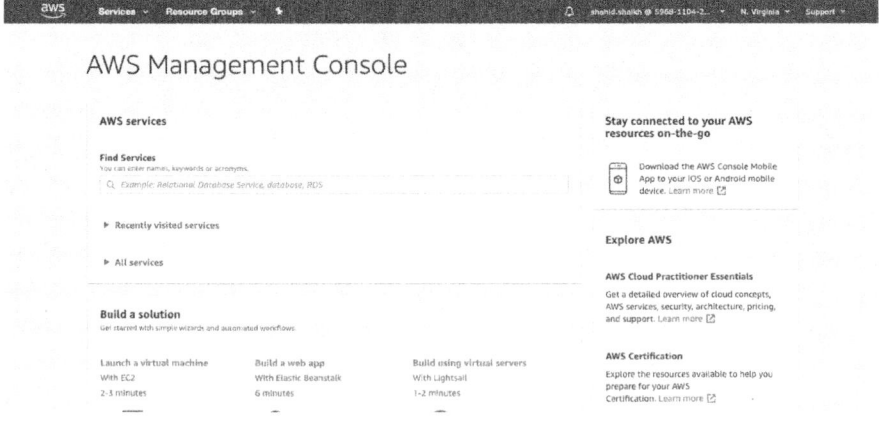

Figure 8.1

2. Search for QLDB and click on it. You should see a screen similar to the one shown here:

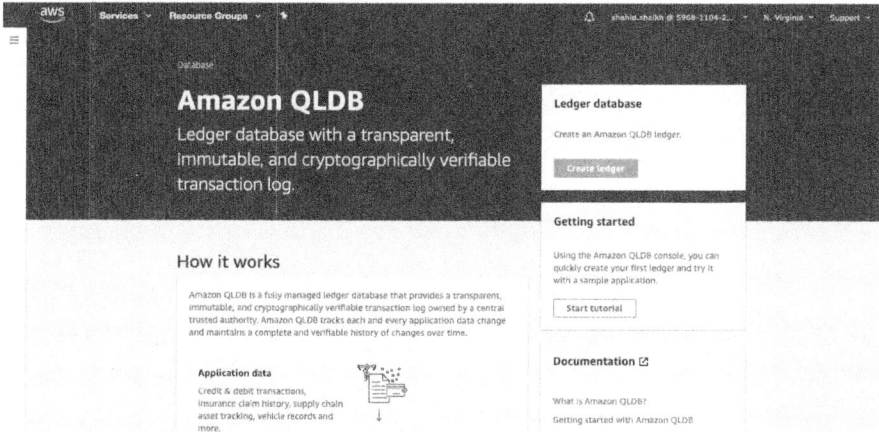

Figure 8.2

3. Click on the **Create ledger** button.
4. Provide the name of the ledger and click on the create button. Once the ledger is created, it should be listed in the ledger screen:

Figure 8.3

5. Click on your ledger name and then click on the **Query editor** from the left menu. It should open a screen similar to the following one:

Figure 8.4

6. Now, run this query to create a new table in the ledger:

   CREATE TABLE users

7. Paste the query in the query editor and click on the Run button. It should create a new table.

8. Now, let's add some information in the table. Copy/paste the following query:

   INSERT into users VALUE {'id': 1, 'name': 'Shahid', 'location': 'Mumbai'}

9. Great. Now, let's fetch some information from our table. Run the following query to fetch records:

   select * from users

   It will return the information present in the table.

10. Let's perform the update query and observe the changes in the QLDB.

11. Run the following query to update the record:

    UPDATE users as u SET u.name='ShahidShaikh' where u.id=1

12. Upon the successful query execution, it will return the ID of the document. Copy the ID.

Let's query the changes and see the history of the record.

1. To retrieve the history of the record, we use the `history()` syntax. Here's the query:

   `select * from history(users) as h where h.metadata.id='id from the update query'`

   This query should return the history of changes made toward the document identified using the ID.

   In my case, here's the output:

Figure 8.5

2. Similarly, you can delete the record from the ledger. Copy/paste and run the following query:

   `DELETE from users as u where u.id=1`

   Similarly, if you run the history query, you will see the deleted record as well in the history log.

Let's check out the various drivers available for Amazon QLDB to perform the integration.

Amazon QLDB Drivers

Amazon QLDB provides the drivers for the following programming languages:

- Java
- Python
- Node.js

.NETAdditionally, you need the Amazon SDK to bring the AWS common functionality required for integration with the QLDB.

Let's install the SDK for Node.js:
1. Create a new folder and switch to it using the Terminal:
   `$ mkdir qldbtest && cd qldbtest`
2. Create a package.Json file using the npm init command:
   `$ npm init --y`
3. Install the QLDB driver using the following command:
   `$ npm install amazon-qldb-driver-nodejs@1.0.0 --save`
4. Install the dependencies drivers:

   `$ npm install aws-sdk --save`

   `$ npm install ion-js@4.0.0 --save`

   `$ npm install jsbi@3.1.2 --save`
5. Once the driver is installed, we can perform the connection. Refer to the following sample:

   ```
   const qldb = require('amazon-qldb-driver-nodejs');
   const main = function() {
   const driver = new qldb.QldbDriver('quick-start', {});
   });
   main();
   ```

We are connecting to the default QLDB ledger that does not require any additional configuration.There you go, we have not made a connection to our QLDB ledger database. You can refer to the documentation page for more information about the drivers and visit this link mentioned.—link to the **Amazon QLDB driver documentation**.

Conclusion

Amazon QLDB is a promising database with an enterprise-grade solution. Amazon QLDB can be used to develop many applications that require ledger - virtually every major application.

In the next chapter, we will learn about the decentralized application already making its way into the mainstream.

Decentralized Apps and Frameworks

CHAPTER 9
OpenBazaar

OpenBazaar is the world's first decentralized peer-to-peer marketplace application. It is an open-source project and can be used by anyone to set up a simple restriction-free, decentralized e-commerce application.

Structure

In this chapter, we will learn the following:
- Introduction to OpenBazaar
- Features of OpenBazaar
- How to install OpenBazaar

Objectives

After reading this chapter, you will be able to:
- Understand the OpenBazaar decentralized application
- Know the features of OpenBazaar
- Install and use OpenBazaar

Let's begin.

Introduction to OpenBazaar

OpenBazaar is an open-source, decentralized, customizable, peer-to-peer application to set up your e-commerce application with no intermediary and no platform fees.

Here's the sample home page of OpenBazaar:

Figure 9.1

OpenBazaar has the following uses:

- You can set up your self-hosted e-commerce application.
- It's a peer to peer, so you can increase your peers to support the demand as your business grows.
- There is no platform fee, as you are the sole owner of the application.
- You can pay via cryptocurrency to make it more secure and convenient.

You can either host your application or join the existing platform running on zokos.com.

Let's learn more about OpenBazaar by studying its features.

Features of OpenBazaar

OpenBazaar is a revolutionary software for the decentralized application space. With this e-commerce platform, people can use their cryptocurrency to buy goods directly from the supplier, so it's spreading the use of cryptocurrency and a decentralized application in the market.

Let's look at the features in detail.

Commission-free

OpenBazaar is an open-source application and runs as a decentralized application. When someone purchases something from a store, they don't have to pay commission he/she has because trade occurs on the peer-to-peer network.

Easy to Set Up

Setting up your store on your server is a difficult task, and if you don't have such experience, you might need to hire someone for the installation and probably support it as well in the future.

Setting up OpenBazaar is very easy. You just need to download the application and run the installer in your system. You can start listing and see your product in the marketplace in no time.

We will do the simple installation of our own in the next section.

Search

OpenBazaar provides built-in search for a vast number of products so that one can search, explore, and buy the products. You can also filter the products based on shipping location, ratings, and other filters.

Built-in Bitcoin Payment Support

OpenBazaar supports Bitcoin by default. You can use Bitcoin to purchase goods and earn Bitcoin by selling goods. It's secure, private, and owned by you.

Conflict Resolution Using Mutually Agreed on Escrow

This is a unique feature that allows both sellers and buyers to reach a consensus and select a third user as an escrow before starting a transaction. This escrow is also a user in the network.

Once the first party submits Bitcoin to the escrow and trade takes place, Bitcoin can only be released after the signatures of all the parties involved in the transaction, making it a secure and independent escrow mechanism.

Built-in Inventory Management

OpenBazaar manages the inventory by default. As and when purchases are made, the inventory is updated automatically so that procurement can begin whenever required.

Multiple Shipping Options

You can provide multiple shipping options to the buyer with different shipping methods and prices so that they can choose as per their convenience.

Order Management

OpenBazaar provides simple yet useful order management features to manage your order anytime and anywhere.

Built-in Live Chat

OpenBazaar provides built-in secure and encrypted chat software so that users can communicate with the seller about the product.

Let's learn about the installation of OpenBazaar.

How to Install OpenBazaar

You can install OpenBazaar in your system by performing the following steps:
- Download the pre-built installation package
- Build the installation from source

I would recommend installing the OpenBazaar by downloading the pre-built software package. Perform the following steps:
1. Navigate to the downloads page of OpenBazaar and choose the installation version based on your operating system.

2. Download the installer and run it:

Figure 9.2

3. Drag and drop the file in the **Applications** folder and run it.
4. On the first run, this is how OpenBazaar application looks:

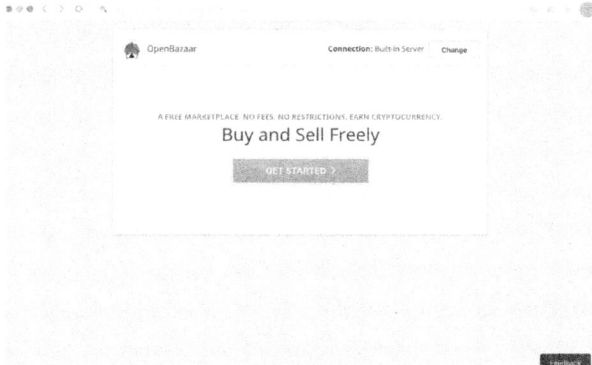

Figure 9.3

5. Click on the **GET STARTED** button and fill up the basic information:

Figure 9.4

6. Agree to the terms and conditions, and you should be able to view your custom store.

You can also search and find items to buy using Bitcoin:

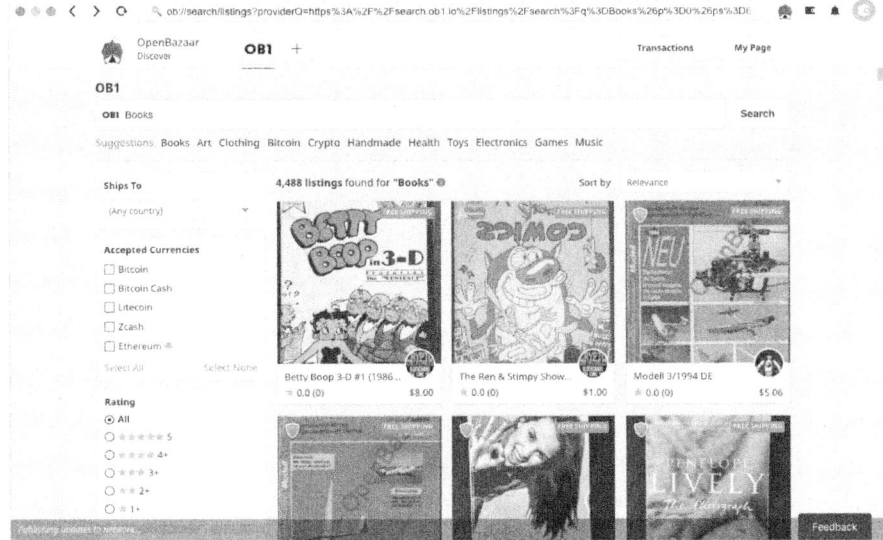

Figure 9.5

There you go! You have your custom peer-to-peer e-commerce platform running on your machine.

Conclusion

OpenBazaar is a revolutionary software and the world's first decentralized application running on a peer-to-peer network. It sets the path of the new generic application development. In the next chapter, we will study another revolutionary decentralized application.

CHAPTER 10
DTube

DTube is a decentralized version of YouTube. It's a video hosting service managed by the network and peers instead of a centralized authority. DTube provides content creators to earn cryptocurrency without showing ads. So, there is no tracking, privacy concerns, and moderations that we have in the existing services.

Structure

In this chapter, we will learn the following:
- Introduction to DTube
- Features of DTube
- DTube Architecture
- How DTube works

Objective

After reading this chapter, you should be able to:
- Know the basics of DTube

- Understand the features of DTube
- Know the technologies that run DTube

Let's begin.

Introduction to DTube

DTube is the world's first decentralized video hosting service. It is an ads-free and fair platform for content creators and viewers.

You can visit DTube by clicking on *DTube* website:

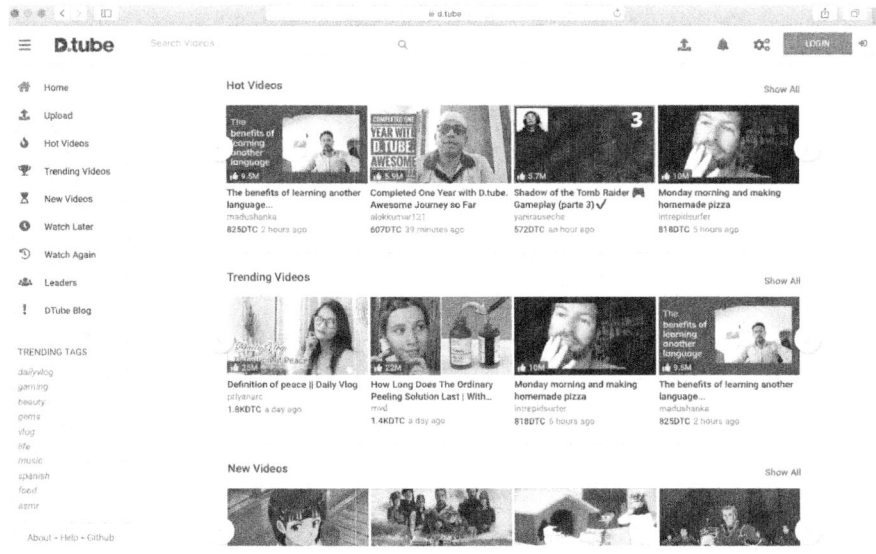

Figure 10.1

DTube runs on the Steem blockchain and stores content on IPFS. We have studied IPFS in detail; let's understand the Steem blockchain in a nutshell.

Steem Blockchain

Steem is a social blockchain network that allows users to create content and get paid for it without showing ads. Steem mints its cryptocurrency coin and shares it with the content creator and users who engage with the content via upvotes or comments.

It also allows developers to build their applications on top of Steem blockchain. DTube uses Steem blockchain to provide content creators with the opportunity to create content and get paid for it without showing ads.

Click on *Steem* Website to visit the website and learn more about it.

DTube uses IPFS to store content. It also shows the power of distributed file storage service that can play a major role in applications like video hosting services.

As a user, you can create an account on DTube and watch videos. You can upvote videos, comment on them, and earn cryptocurrency for that engagement.

Let's check out the features of DTube.

Features of DTube

DTube has the following features for consumers and content creators:
- Content ownership to the content creator.
- Zero moderation and censorship.
- Payment based on the engagement on the content.
- Payment to content consumers based on engagement.
- Zero transaction fees.
- Decentralized content storage using IPFS.
- Channel creation, subscription, and alerts are similar to YouTube.
- Minimal learning curve due to features' similarity with YouTube.

Let's understand the architecture of DTube.

DTube Architecture

DTube employs multiple technologies to make the site work, and the architecture consists of the following technologies:
- **Front-end:** JavaScript Meteor framework
- **Distributed Blockchain Database:** Avalon
- **Media Storage:** Steem and IPFS

Let's learn, in brief, about the architecture components of DTube.

Front-end

DTube front-end is built on HTML,CSS, and JavaScript. It uses a popular JavaScript framework called Meteor to build single-page applications.

Distributed Blockchain Database

DTube uses a distributed database called Avalon. It's a database built for blockchain-based applications, and it is built specifically for social networking applications like DTube.

Media Storage

DTube uses IPFS and Steem to manage storage. It uses IPFS to store content in the network and Steem to record the engagement on the content created by the user.

Let's understand how DTube works.

How DTube Works

In DTube, you can create your account and start watching videos, just like on YouTube.

The only difference here is that you don't see ads. As a content consumer, if you upvote a video and become part of the conversation in the comments, you're paid based on how valuable your contribution to the content is.

As a content creator, you can create your channel and upload your content. You get paid based on how good your content is and how many people are engaged in the form of views, votes, comments.

Might the question arise, though? Where is the cryptocurrency coming from? Well, Steem blockchain mints new Steem coins every 24 hours to distribute it to the network.

DTube uses Avalon blockchain to store the content uploaded to the site. Along with Avalon blockchain, it uses IPFS to store static files such as videos, photos, features, and images.

DTube has its coin called **DTube Coin (DTC)**. Avalon blockchain mints DTC every day to distribute it to the users, and it's called a reward pool.

Content creators are paid based on the engagement on the content, and engagement such as page views, votes, and comments decide the payments in the form of DTC.

In a nutshell, this is how DTube works. DTube is an open-source project, and you can check out the source code at *DTube Github*.

Conclusion

DTube is a very interesting and user-friendly decentralized application. It uses technologies that we are already familiar with and provides a safe and content-focused alternative to YouTube.

In the next chapter, we will learn about the Ocean protocol—a decentralized marketplace to exchange data.

CHAPTER 11
Ocean Protocol

Ocean Protocol is a decentralized data exchange protocol developed for information exchange by people and earn cryptocurrency to either sell or consume data. Ocean protocol developed the decentralized way to buy/sell data with a focus on privacy.

Structure

In this chapter, we will cover the following topics:
- Introduction to Ocean protocol
- Use cases of Ocean protocol
- How does Ocean protocol work?
- Ocean architecture

Objective

After reading this chapter, you will be able to:
- Understand the basics of Ocean protocol
- Learn how Ocean protocol works

Introduction to Ocean Protocol

Do you know the largest assets in the market? You probably think real estate, stocks, oil, and maybe water as well.

However, the biggest asset in the world right now is data. Yes, you heard it right. As the saying goes:

Data is the new oil

But who owns data? I guess you already know the answer. It's Google, Facebook, and other so-called free services that own the data generated by you. They use this data to train their algorithms or, worse, manipulate voters in the election (read about the **Cambridge analytica** scandal in the United States 2016 election to get in-depth information).

These large conglomerates don't share this data with parties that need it. For example, a cancer researcher can use such data to perform a predictive analysis. It's almost impossible to find as much data as these companies possess.

Ocean Protocol is developed to tackle this problem. It provides a secure and privacy-focused platform to exchange data with monetary benefits. Data owners can share data by keeping the privacy, and data consumers can access data after paying the owner the requested amount in cryptocurrency.

You can use Ocean protocol to set up your marketplace that enables users to buy/sell data. Ocean protocol will manage the security and privacy of the transaction.

Let's learn about the features of the Ocean protocol.

Use Cases of Ocean Protocol

Ocean protocol can be used in a variety of applications. Here are a few examples:

Autonomous Vehicles

Manufacturers of autonomous cars require lots of data to train the artificial intelligence program that drives the car.

Organizations assume that they need at least 500 million to 1 billion miles driven records to train the algorithm so that it can drive safely on roads and make accurate decisions.

Ocean protocol can be used to develop a marketplace where individual drivers can submit their data and get paid for it. Car manufacturers can use the data to train the algorithms.

Medical Research

Tons of researchers require data to finish their research. At the time of writing this book, we are dealing with the COVID19 pandemic, and almost every biotechnology company is on a deadline to develop a vaccine to make humans immune to this virus.

The only way researchers can figure this out is by using data, which can help researchers make very effective decisions.

Ocean protocol aims exactly toward situations like this, where people who own data get paid for sharing it privately with researchers.

Global Datastore

Ocean protocol can be used to build a global data store where almost all data related to technology, science, virology, and medicines is available and developers can easily use it to build/train algorithms.

Let's understand how ocean protocol works.

How Does Ocean Protocol Work?

Let's understand how ocean protocol works. There are three main actors in the protocol:
- Data providers
- Data marketplace
- Data consumers

Let's understand each of these.

Data Providers

If you own some data and want to sell it, you are a **data provider**. A data provider is a legal custodian of data.

For example, you might be using a fitness watch, or you know someone who uses a fitness watch. They use a watch for a specific period, say a month, and that generates lots of data about the body such as sleep time, heartbeats, and so on.

Now, suppose you want to sell this data. First, you need to generate and upload the data on some service such as Google drive, dropbox, and so on.

Once you have the free link of the data, you can hook it up with Ocean protocol and place it in the marketplace.

Ocean protocol never stores your actual data;it stores the metadata of your records and puts it in the marketplace.Ocean protocol handles the security of the metadata so that there is no breach of privacy.

Data Marketplace

You are ready to sell the data, so you can list it in the third-party data marketplace built using ocean protocol. The data marketplace then lists your data, and it's ready for the consumer.

Data Consumer

A data consumer is an entity that uses your data to build their applications, train their algorithms, and so on. Ocean protocol manages the data and ensures that the consumer has paid the amount listed in the metadata.

Once a customer has paid the amount, they will have access to the data, and the provider will be paid an amount in cryptocurrency.

For detailed information, you can visit the ocean protocol official website.

Link to the official ocean website: Ocean website

Let's understand the ocean protocol architecture.

Ocean Protocol Architecture

Here's the ocean protocol architecture diagram by the Ocean protocol team:

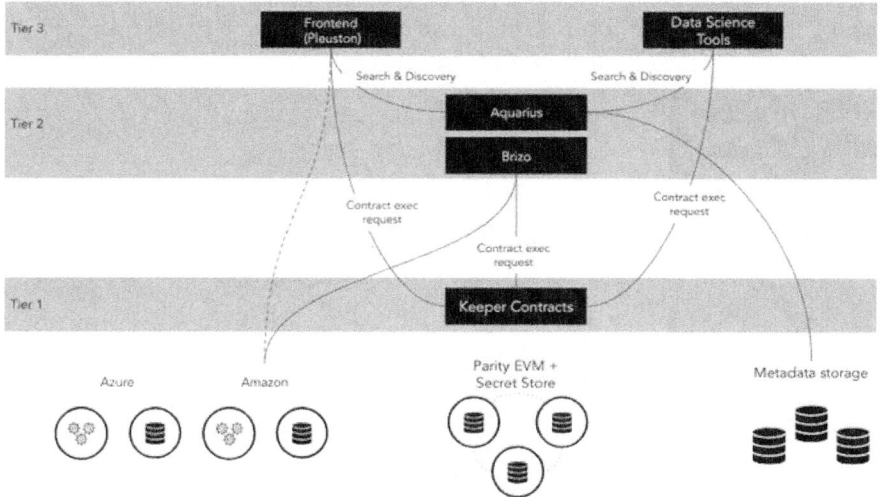

Figure 11.1

Ocean protocol consists of the following tiers:
- Smart contracts - Tier 1
- Protocol layer - Tier 2
- Front-end layer - Tier 3

Tier 1

Tier 1 consists of the ocean protocol smart contracts that can be executed on any Ethereum virtual machine.

Tier 2

Tier 2 consists of high-level libraries and protocols to deal with the front-end and smart contracts tiers.

Tier 2 consists of the following sub-components:
- **Squid:** It's a high-level API that interacts with ocean components.

- **Aquarius:** It manages the metadata. It is written in Python.
- **Brizo:** It interacts with the cloud services to manage the actual content.

Tier 3

Tier 3 is a front-end application that provides a user interface to perform various actions such as publishing data on the marketplace.

Front-end tier consists of HTML, CSS, and React.

The user interacts with the front-end layer to perform the data exchange.

Conclusion

Ocean protocol is the revolutionary software that allows users to own their data and give access to those they trust. It allows users to publish their data and earn incentives once it is consumed. It brings back control of the data where it belongs—with you, the user.

In the next chapter, we will look at DTube and its architecture.

Index

A

Amazon Ion 152
Amazon QLDB
  about 150
  drivers 157, 158
  usage 154-157
Amazon QLDB, features
  about 151
  cryptographically secure 152
  enterprise-grade 152
  high availability 152
  immutable 151
  ledger database 151
  SQL compatible query
    language 152

Amazon QLDB, use cases
  about 153
  finance 153
  insurance 153
  manufacturing 153
  payroll system 153
  supply chain 154
asymmetric cryptography 4
audit trails 130
Avalon database 170

B

BigchainDB
  about 124
  blockchain features 124
  database features 124
  decentralization 125
  high transaction rate 127

identity management 129
immutability 125, 126
intellectual property rights management 129
low latency and fast finality 127
owner-controlled assets 126
structured data, indexing and querying 127
supply chain 128
use cases 128
BigchainDB node
 running 130-132
Bitcoin
 about 7, 14, 15, 37
 working 15-17
bits 21
block
 about 9, 19
 block header 9
 Nonce 9
 transactions 9
Blockchain
 about 2, 26
 basics 3
 characteristics 4
 core components 7
 federated Blockchain 5
 history 6, 7
 private Blockchain 5
 public Blockchain 5
 types 4
 working 8
block header
 bits 19
 merkle root 19
 nonce 19
 previous block hash 19
 time 19
 version 19
Bluzelle 142
Bluzelle, entities
 consumer 142
 producer 142
Bluzelle, features
 about 142
 affordable 143
 decentralized 143
 global coverage 143
 mutable 143
 shared revenue model 144
Bluzelle Native Token (BNT) 145
Bluzelle node
 setting up 147, 148
Bluzelle technology 144
Bluzelle technology, components
 Bluzelle tokens 145
 client library and proxy 146
 consensus engine 145
 database engine 144
 nodes 145
 zone 145
Bluzelle tokens
 types 145
Bluzelle, use cases
 about 146
 currency exchange markets 146

Index

data streaming networks 146
prediction markets 146
Byzantine Fault
  Tolerance (BFT) 14

C

Candidate block 9
chain 10, 11
command parameter, Testnet Blockchain
  --syncmode 45
  --testnet 45
Conflict-free Replicated Data Types (CRDTs) 102
consensus algorithms 12
consensus algorithms, types
  proof of stake (POS) 13, 14
  proof of work 13
consensus mechanism 13
content-based addressing 69
content discovery 94
contract structure
  about 52
  Enum data types 54
  events 54
  function modifier 53
  functions 53
  state variables 53
  structure (Struct) 54
counter data model 107

D

DApps Protocols 29, 30
DApps stack
  about 62
  front-end 62
  smart contracts 62, 63
  storage 63
data definition 32
data governance 130
data layer 32, 33
decentralization 26
decentralized applications (DApps)
  about 26-28, 40, 41
  advantage 61
  building, with OrbitDB 107-109
  components 40
  with Ethereum 59
  working 28, 29
Decentralized approach 26
Decentralized Message Communications Protocols 66
Direct Acyclic Graph (DAG) 70
Distributed Hash Table (DHT)
  about 70, 71
  advantages 70
docs data model 106, 107
double spending issue 17, 18
DTube
  about 168
  architecture 169
  features 169
  working 170, 171
DTube, architecture technologies
  distributed blockchain database 170
  front-end 170
  media storage 170

E

electronic cash system 17
end-to-end encryption 94
enum data types 54
escrow 163, 164
Ethash 40
Ethereum
  about 36, 37, 41, 40
  Blockchain 36
  Ether 36
  globally distributed infrastructure 36
  history 38, 39
  open source project 36
  peer to peer 36
  projects 60
  smart contracts 36
  using, in decentralized applications (DApps) 59
Ethereum client 41, 42
Ethereum components
  about 39
  clients 40
  consensus algorithm 40
  data structure 40
  peer-to-peer (P2P) network 39
  state machine 40
  transactions 40
Ethereum Name Service (ENS) 66
Ethereum network
  about 42
  testnet 42
Ethereum network, types
  mainnet 42

Ethereum protocol
  programming languages 41, 42
Ethereum white paper
  reference link 38
events 54

F

federated Blockchain 5
feed data model 104, 105
fees 24, 25
Filecoin 33
full-stack App
  building, in backend with IPFS 84-92
function modifier 53
functions 53

G

Ganache
  about 45
  installing 45, 46
  reference link 46
Genesis block 3
Geth
  installing 42-44
Geth, build files
  reference link 43
global IPFS network gateway
  reference link 78

H

hexadecimal number 23

I

identity module 94
identity theft 129
Infura 46-48

Internet of things (IoT) 129
Interplanetary File
    System (IPFS)
  about 29, 64, 68
  command line 75, 76
  configuring 71-75
  features 32
  installing 71-75
  modules 69
  static website,
    hosting in 78, 79, 83
  used, for building full-stack
    App in backend 84-92
  working 68
Interplanetary Linked
    Data (IPLD) 69
IPFS addresses 77
IPFS bootstrap address 77
IPFS Cluster
  about 92, 93
  reference link 93
IPFS command, types
  offline 76
  online 76
IPFS, content-addressing
  reference link 68
IPFS Node
  configuring 76
IPFS stack
  subnet layers 31

J
JavaScript Object
    Notation (JSON) 48, 76
JSON-RPC API 48, 49

K
key-value data model 105

L
Libp2p, components
  about 93
  content discovery 94
  end-to-end encryption 94
  identity module 94
  messaging module 94-98
  routing 94
  transport layer protocol 93
Libp2p project
  about 31, 93
  features 31
log data model 104

M
mainnet 42
Merkle-DAG 70
Merkle tree
  about 19-21
  reference link 21
messaging module 94-98
miners 11, 12

N
naming layer 32
networking layer 31
node 8
Node.js
  reference link 84
Nonce 22

O
Ocean Protocol
  about 174
  architecture 177

data consumer 176
data marketplace 176
data provider 175, 176
  working 175
Ocean Protocol, tiers
  front-end layer 178
  protocol layer 177
  smart contracts 177
Ocean Protocol, use cases
  about 174
  autonomous vehicles 174, 175
  global datastore 175
  medical research 175
OpenBazaar
  about 162
  built-in inventory
    management 164
  built-in live chat 164
  installation 164-166
  multiple shipping options 164
  order management 164
  uses 162
OpenBazaar, features
  about 162
  Bitcoin 163
  built-in search 163
  commission-free 163
  easy to set up 163
OrbitDB
  about 68, 102
  installing 103
  technologies 110
  used, for building
    DApps 107-109

OrbitDB data models
  about 104
  counter data model 107
  docs data model 106, 107
  feed data model 104, 105
  key-value data model 105
  log data model 104

P

PartiQL 152
peer-to-peer email application
  architecture 110-121
peer-to-peer hypermedia
  protocol 32
private Blockchain 5
proof of stake (POS) 13, 14
proof of work 13
protocol layer, sub-components
  Aquarius 178
  Brizo 178
  Squid 177
public Blockchain 5

R

Remote Procedure
  Call (RPC) 48
routing 94

S

SHA256 algorithm 21
SHA-256 function 13
Simple Message Transfer
  Protocol (SMTP) 110
smart contracts 29, 50, 51
solidity data types
  about 51, 52
  address 52
  arrays 52

Boolean 51
enum 52
fixed point 52
integer 52
mapping 52
struct 52
solidity language 50, 51
solidity language, installation instructions
  reference link 51
solidity program
  writing 54-59
state variables 53
static website
  hosting, in IPFS 78, 79, 83
Steem Blockchain 168, 169
Structure (Struct) 54
Swarm
  about 64-66
  reference link 64

T

Testnet Blockchain
  synchronizing 44, 45
testnet node 42
TiesDB
  about 134
  data organization 135
  features 134
  incentive schemes 135
  security 135
  verified identification 135
TiesDB network, entities
  client 134
  coordinator 134

  node 134
  user 134
TiesDB node
  running 137-139
TiesDB, use cases
  about 135
  big data analytics 137
  distributed datastore 136
  file sharing 136
  intellectual property right management 136
  mass media 136
  social network 137
Torrent network 27
transaction 8, 9, 22
transaction data 24
transaction ID (TXID) 21, 23
transaction payload 24
transport layer protocol 93

U

Unspent Transaction Output (UTXO) 25, 26

V

VSCode
  reference link 55

W

WebRTC 31
weight 25

Z

zones, Bluzelle network nodes
  database zone 145
  hub zone 145
  peg zone 145

Printed in Great Britain
by Amazon